INTERLINK ILLUSTRATED HISTORIES

Middle East Conflicts

D1017988

INTERLINK ILLUSTRATED HISTORIES

MIDDLE **E**AST

CONFLICTS

FRANÇOIS MASSOULIÉ

Translated by Angela Parker

Interlink Books
An imprint of Interlink Publishing Group, Inc.
New York • Northampton

This edition first published in 2003 by

INTERLINK BOOKS
An imprint of Interlink Publishing Group, Inc.
99 Seventh Avenue · Brooklyn, New York 11215 and
46 Crosby Street · Northampton, Massachusetts 01060

Library of Congress Cataloging-in-Publication Data
Massoulié, François.
  [Conflits du Proche-Orient. English]
  Middle East conflicts / François Massoulié.
    p. cm. — (Interlink illustrated histories)
  includes bibliographic references (p.) and index
  ISBN 1-56656-237-6
    1. Middle East—Politics and government—20th century. I. Title.
  II. Series.
  DS62.8.M3213 2003
  956.9405–dc21   98-20065
                                                        CIP

Typeset by Archetype IT Ltd.
Printed and bound in Italy

Rooted at a nexus of contending empires, rival religions, competing trade routes, and sought-after resources, it is not surprising that the history of the Middle East is riven with the conflicts of history. The 20th century alone has witnessed the colonial division into nation-states of the vast Arab nation that once stretched unbroken from the Mediterranean to the Gulf of Oman and from Aleppo in the north to the southern Yemeni port of Aden. That century alone brought the defeat of Ottoman and British imperial rule and their eventual replacement by US domination; the arrival of Zionist pioneers followed by European Jewish survivors and their ascension to power with the founding of Israel; the expulsion of what would become generations of suddenly landless refugees in Palestine's *al-Nakba* (catastrophe) of 1948; the creation and collapse of Iran's short-lived Pahlavi "dynasty"; the discovery of vast lakes of oil beneath the least populated and suddenly staggeringly wealthy parts of the region. We watched regional crises of power turn into battles of clan and religion within states, in places like Lebanon and Yemen, while Israel's occupations of Palestine as well as other Arab lands kept the region at or over the brink of war. We saw the Arab world's emerging unity collapse in the ashes of Iraq's invasion of Kuwait and Operation Desert Storm. We watched one country's path to Arab nationalism defeated, replaced by the beguiling illusions of Palestinian autonomy, militant Islamism, and the false promise of a vibrant global economy. And as the next century was just settling in, we saw terrorist attacks once thought to be limited to "other" venues strike devastatingly hard, right here in the US. And we watched as Washington responded to those crimes not with an international coalition to find and bring to justice the perpetrators, but with a war without limits, without borders, without end. A war that began in, and began to transform once again, the Middle East.

François Massoulié traces those conflicts—the battles of ideologies and hegemonies, wars and occupations—that have forged the volatile mosaic known as the modern Middle East. The French scholar-diplomat provides a comprehensive, lively account of 20th-century Middle East history, anchored in his years working in the region. In today's post-September-11th world of blazing headlines and hysteria passing for analysis, this coolly analytic look at real history is all the more compelling.

—Phyllis Bennis
fellow, Institute for Policy Studies, and author,
Before & After: US Foreign Policy and the September 11th Crisis

Chapter 1

THE HERITAGE
OF THE PAST

THE MIDDLE EAST IS MADE UP OF THREE DISTINCT AREAS:
EGYPT, THE FERTILE CRESCENT, AND THE ARAB PENINSULA. FOR
CENTURIES IT HAS BEEN CRISS-CROSSED BY ARMIES AND CARAVANS
OF DESERT TRADERS...

I n 5 BC the Greek historian Herodotus declared that "Egypt was a gift from the Nile." In a largely desert country, life has always been organized around this major river. From the Sudanese borders to the marshes of the delta the *fellahs*, the local peasants, practiced an irrigation culture and their lives were governed by the rising water and the two annual harvests. These geographical conditions favored political and territorial unity. In turn, the Pharaohs, the Greeks, the Romans, the Byzantines and the Arabs have all realized this. They knew that whoever held the capital – whether it be Memphis, Thebes, Alexandria or Cairo – controlled Egypt. From there the Pharaohs and the Sultans could further their ambitions in deeper Africa, or turn their attention beyond the Sinai desert peninsula toward the Asiatic shores of the Mediterranean.

The Fertile Crescent which was once Mesopotamia and now mostly Iraq and Syria, is altogether different. It forms a link between the Eastern Mediterranean and the Indian Ocean, and between Europe and Asia, and is an open geographical area which has no natural boundaries. It stretches from Mount Lebanon to the Iranian foothills and the mountainous areas contrast greatly with landscapes of semi-desert plains. Rising in the plateau of Anatolia, the rivers Tigris and the Euphrates flow diagonally across the Fertile Crescent, but their waters, which ebb and flow erratically, are poorly exploited and do not irrigate the region in depth.

The oldest known urban concentrations, Ur, Babylon,

The Ottoman Citadel, which was built on the spur of the Moqattam hill completely dominates Cairo, the town of a thousand minarets. It was here that Mehmet Ali invited the Mamluks to a great banquet, and as they left all the members of this military caste were massacred.
Ph. © LL-Viollet

Nineveh, and Ctesiphon were created here. But each of these civilizations foundered after a few centuries, exhausted by internecine rivalries, or defeated by foreign invaders. However, both the powerful Persian dynasties of the Achaemenids (sixth to fourth century BC) and the Sassanids (third to seventh century AD) managed to retain control of Mesopotamia, the western border of their empire. As it looked out over the Mediterranean, the Fertile Crescent found itself equally at the mercy of Western conquerors: the Greeks and the Romans. This region has been criss-crossed for centuries by armies and caravans of desert traders.

The third area, the Arab peninsula, where travellers avoided the vast desert stretches, was set apart from these struggles for supremacy. But as still and empty as the region appeared to outsiders, it actually pulsed with its own dynamic internal forces. The coastal population who had Sudanese Africa to the west and Persia to the east were very different from the tribes of the interior. The Arab peninsula controlled the East African, and most importantly, the Indian Ocean shipping routes by

means of the Bab-el-Mandeb and Hormuz Straits. This geopolitical constant was steadily to assume a fundamental importance, which increased in the nineteenth century after the opening of the Suez Canal. It was here that the Bedouin contested borders with the more sedentary population. In their own way the Bedouin contributed to the general economy of the Middle East, but their diverse politics, characteristic of their tribal way of life, prevented them from participating in the struggle being waged by opposing political leaders for regional domination.

Until 1964 when the Aswan high dam was built, Egypt was at the mercy of the two annual floods. Today these flooded landscapes have disappeared. Ph. © LL-Viollet

Mohammad and the Arab Muslim Empire

It was on the Arab peninsula that the great politico-religious force of Islam came into being. Its message of unity was initially addressed to the Arab tribes of the peninsula. Mohammad united them in one great, common objective: the dissemination of the newly-received faith. In the space of ten years the Prophet extended the power of Islam across all Arabia. As Mecca was situated at the axis of the two great caravan routes which crossed the peninsula, it proved a meeting point for all the tribes. The Ka'ba stood there. This sacred black stone had been worshipped by the Arabs for years and Mohammad made it the symbol of Islam. The prayers of the faithful, modelled on earlier Jewish prayers toward

"In the name of God, the Beneficent, the Merciful." The classic calligraphic text of the first verse of the Qur'an.
Ph. © Edimedia

Jerusalem, soon turned to Mecca.

By the time of the Prophet's death his troops were already preparing to mount an attack on Byzantine Syria to expand their religion's influence. This undertaking seemed timely as the Byzantine and Sassanian Empires appeared exhausted by their struggle for supremacy. What is more, Islam had won the favor of the "People of the Book." Jews, Sabines, Christians and Zoroastrians benefited from a privileged status: if they paid a special tax, the *jizya*, they were allowed to practice their religion and administer their own communities.

In 634 a decisive victory opened Jerusalem, Damascus and Egypt to the Muslim army. The following year the Battle of Qadisiya precipitated the collapse of the Persian Empire and delivered Mesopotamia to the Byzantine governors. The Middle East, which was shaped by the four successive capitals of Arab-Muslim power – Mecca, Damascus, Baghdad and Cairo – formed the heart of an empire which in the space of a century would stretch from the Pyrenees to the Hindu Kush. The whole culture soon became overwhelmingly Arabic-speaking.

The Abbasid dynasty, successors to Mohammad, overthrew the Umayyads in 750 and moved the capital from Damascus to Baghdad in the Fertile Crescent. This gave rise to the historical rivalry between Damascus and Baghdad. The new capital, which was a trading cross-

WAR ACCORDING TO IBN KHALDUN

There have always been wars. War first came about from a desire for vengeance. Each adversary is backed by his own people. The thirst for vengeance is normally driven by jealousy, envy, hatred, religious fervor, or by devotion to the royal cause, or by attempts to found a dynasty. The first type of war normally erupts between neighboring tribes or rival families.

The second type, caused by hatred is carried out by savage desert tribes like the nomadic Arabs, the Turks, the Turkomans, the Kurds and people like them. They find a point to their lives through warfare and live on the spoils of others...

The third type of war is the *jihad*, the Holy War according to religious law. And the fourth and last is the "dynastic war" against dissidents and rebels. Those are the four kinds of war. The first two are unjust and iniquitous: the second two are just and holy wars. ■

Ibn Khaldun (1332–1406), quoted in Sinbad's *Discourse on World History.* 1978. 554–555.

roads between the Mediterranean world to the west and India and China to the east, became a center of learning. While the West could scarcely repel barbarian invasions, the caliphate of Harun al-Rashid, legendary hero of *The Thousand and One Nights,* was representative of a forward-looking civilization.

At the heart of Mecca stands the black stone of the Ka'ba, the symbol which had already been worshipped by the Arabs of the jahiliyya "the age of ignorance" which preceded the revelations of the Qur'an.
Ph. © Boyer/Viollet

The Ottoman Solution (1453–1918)

In the sixteenth century, the Ottomans, Sunni Turks who came from the steppes of Central Asia, created an empire whose ideological justification and political cement was Islam. The only exception was Persia which embraced Shi'ism. The Ottoman Empire was to leave a lasting impression on the Middle East which it ruled in many forms right up to modern times. To counter the many divisions in the region, what came to be called the "Ottoman Solution" concentrated on developing the perfect denationalized Islamic state. Unlike earlier caliphates, the Ottomans did not immerse themselves in Arab culture. Indeed Turkish became the administrative language of this huge empire which straddled Europe and Asia. The Sultan ruled a military force from Istanbul which included Jews, Christians and Muslims. There was little central interference in the internal affairs of the people. Religious communities (based in regions

The irrigation systems on the Tigris, which had been perfected since Babylonian times, made Mesopotamia's fortune. But at the beginning of the twentieth century the fasti of the Abbasid Caliphate revolted and Baghdad became a mere provincial capital lost on the borders of the Ottoman Empire, and left alone to face the Persian enemy.
Ph © L'Illustration/Sygma

or villages), guilds and tribes were all collectively responsible and each kept its individual characteristics and its autonomy. Local dynasties, some of which had been established before the Ottoman Conquest, such as the Emirs of Kurdistan or the Mamluks of Egypt, continued to exist in the shadow of Istanbul. Patriarchs and Rabbis became very influential and were given broad-ranging jurisdiction in their own communities. It was the same for the Muslims, except that the *ulamas* played a rather more important political role. Supposedly supervising the application of Islamic law, the *Shari'a*, they were in fact the principle link between the Sultan and the people, and they justified his initiatives in the name of common interest.

The Turkish Sultan, who was a stranger to the Arab Middle East, drew his legitimacy from his ability to fight against the Christian powers and the Shi'ites, to defend the holy places and organize pilgrimages to Mecca and Medina. The idea of nationality which implied a relatively homogenous population, remained totally alien to

Ottoman political philosophy. As the guarantor of Sunni orthodoxy the Sultan had to find some way to include all believers under his protection whether they were Turks, Arabs or whatever. Following the logic of its political beliefs the Ottoman Empire happily left the protection of its non-Muslim subjects to foreign powers. This was the so-called system of Capitulations: foreign powers (such as France for the Catholics of what is today's Lebanon) extended protection from the Sultan's jurisdiction to specific sectors of the population. It was largely because of this system that the Europeans were able to hasten their seizure of this colossal empire which in the eighteenth century became known as "the sick man of Europe."

In 1683 the failure of the Great Turk's armies in Vienna, against the German-Roman empire and a coalition of Christian princes, marked the beginning of Ottoman decline. From the eighteenth century onwards Russia moved toward establishing a warm water port and seized Caucasia from Istanbul. The Empire was under threat in Europe where the Greeks were claiming independence, and it also saw the Arab West weakening. In 1830 the King of France, Charles X, expelled the Ottoman Bey of Algeria and occupied the country. The Ottoman Empire retrenched and centered around Anatolia and its eastern Arab provinces. But danger soon threatened the historic heart of the Empire, the Arab peninsula, which had been shaken by internal feuding.

After the time of the Umayyads the Arab peninsula returned to its ancestral divisions. Neither the Ottomans nor their predecessors had really tried to rule this region, except for its fringes: Hijaz, of course, site of the holy places, and Yemen. In the eighteenth century the meeting between a religious preacher, Abd al-Wahhab, and a tribal chief, Ibn Saud, revived the unitarian dynamic of the peninsula. Wahhabism advocated a return to a more rigorous Islam. It was opposed to all Shi'ite heresies, but also to corrupt Ottoman customs and to the dominance of the Sunni. In 1744 the first Wahhabite state was established by the Saud family in Arabia. Its Bedouin troops seized Mecca where they destroyed all idolatrous ornaments.

The Wahhabite movement reached such proportions

Religion has bonded temporal power and religious law and its doctrines, and these are in the interest of civilization.

Ibn Khaldun

that in 1813 the worried Sultan called on Mehmet Ali, the Egyptian governor, to send troops to repress it. In 1818 and 1836 Mehmet Ali crushed the Wahhabites, and they were driven back to central Arabia for half a century.

At the same time, in opposition to Istanbul, Mehmet Ali, a Janissary warrior caste mercenary of Albanian origin, lay the foundations of Egyptian nationalism. He nationalized the land, created the first modern printing works, and reorganized the army. His "great plan" to be the founder of modern Egypt was somewhat ambiguous. An apparent Egyptian nationalist, his aspirations were nevertheless directly descended from the Ottoman Empire which he hoped to reunify for his own ends. From 1832 on a series of successful campaigns won him Palestine and Syria. It was only under pressure from Great Britain that he withdrew in 1840.

European Intervention

As well as the internal problems, and the expansionist ambitions of Egypt and Arabia, the weakened Empire also had to deal with growing interference from European powers who were then confirming their interest in the Middle East.

It was the same in the Gulf. After the discovery of the Indian spice route by Vasco da Gama in 1497 the control of the maritime bases on the shores of the Arab peninsula became a major issue.

*M*ehmet Ali (1769–1849), the former Albanian mercenary, was the great reformer of modern Egypt. He was initially encouraged to reform by Bonaparte's Egyptian expedition (1798–1801) which undermined the traditional Mamluk power bases.
Ph © Harlingue/Viollet

In 1639, as part of its broader empire-building efforts to control the seas, Great Britain set up a trading post at Basra, a town in south-east Mesopotamia, which was at the intersection of the Indian Ocean and the land route. Aden, the Red Sea port, was occupied in 1839. As for the Persian Gulf, in 1853 a permanent peace treaty was drawn up with some of the Emirates who then became officially "protected." The "Pirate Coast" became the "Truce Coast."

On his tour of the region in 1903 the Vice Lord of the Admiralty, Lord Curzon, clearly reminded the Emirs of the nature and terms of this truce: it was a question of defending "*our* commerce as well as *your* security." From then on Britain ensured the defense of the Emirates, but by imposing their own strategic requirements of endorsing and protecting local leaders, the British had completely upset the political balance in the region.

Until then the coastal tribal confederations had benefited from the rivalry between the Ottoman Empire and the Persian Safavid Empire as it had allowed them to preserve their autonomy in this border region. They sold their allegiance to the power of the moment and then re-established their independence. This was how, at the beginning of the nineteenth century, the Emirs of Kuwait came to accept the title of *Qaim Maqam*; they became, nominally, employees of the Sublime Porte within the

jurisdiction of the governor of Basra. But in 1899 Kuwait benefited officially from British protection as British mail to and from India passed through the country. This gave some stability to the area and prevented the Germans, allied with Istanbul, from reaching Kuwait. By these means Britain set up borders – where none had existed – and guaranteed the stability of the existing power. This was an artificial stability, which carried with it the seeds of eventual conflict, and which was totally at odds with the traditional delicate socio-political balance. Essentially, the British completely upset the local order, because the weakest were forced to seek its protection and then became the strongest. This is how the small Emirate of Qatar with barely 500,000 inhabitants today has survived the upheavals of the twentieth century. On

On the eve of the First World War, Sultan Mehmet V (1909–1919) reviewed the Ottoman troops in Salonika, now in Greece.
Ph © Harlingue/Viollet

the other hand, the Emirate of Kab is nowadays completely forgotten, although it had a population of over half a million at the beginning of the century. It was absorbed into Iranian Khouzistan at the end of the First World War. Because they were constructed by a logic that was foreign to the region, the survival of the Gulf Emirates was entirely due to external support.

In the nineteenth century, as inter-empire clashes increased and once-closed worlds were opened, the decline of the Ottoman Empire increased in pace. Under pressure from the newer and more dynamic Western powers, the Ottoman Empire tried to modernize, borrowing heavily to do so. The weight of the debt became crippling. By changing the nature of the principle of Capitulations, the Great Powers came to set the rate of customs

duties and thereby managed to control commercial transactions. In 1875–76 when Egypt and the Ottoman states declared that they were bankrupt, European creditors collected a third of the state revenues, from tobacco companies, the salt monopoly, harbor taxes and more. In Egypt Mehmet Ali and his successors who had financed the building of the Suez Canal – which opened in 1869 – were forced to sell their shares to the British. So the Egyptian state did not share in the benefits of the Canal which soon became of primary economic and strategic importance. In 1882 Britain occupied Egypt "on a temporary basis" to suppress the nationalist movement of Colonel Orabi and its troops set up camp on the banks of the Suez Canal. In 1899 Britain set up Anglo-Egyptian control of the Sudan. At the

***B**uilt on the two banks of the Bosphorus, Istanbul is a bridge between Asia and Europe. Serbs, Albanians, Macedonians, Greeks, Turks, Armenians, Jews, Kurds and Arabs have all contributed to the prosperity of the city. Istanbul was occupied by the Allies in 1918 and passed over by Mustafa Kemal when he chose the Anatolian town of Ankara to be the capital of the new nation.*
Ph © Collection Viollet

Dug by the French engineer Ferdinand de Lesseps, the Suez Canal was opened in 1869 and then placed under international control after Egypt went bankrupt. It was not until 1956 that Nasser nationalized the Universal Canal Company.
Ph © LL. Viollet

beginning of the twentieth century, because of the economic, cultural and political concessions which had been wrested from them, the Ottoman Empire was in fact divided into spheres of influence. With the development of modern shipping, oil became important. Known for centuries as *naft* in the Arab World, oil took on as much an economic as a strategic stake in the industrialized world. Both the Germans and the British tried to obtain concessions for their respective companies from the Ottomans. Their opposing interests were paradoxically linked in the Turkish Petroleum Company which was allowed to drill for oil in Mesopotamia. This agreement was only one of numerous pieces of the puzzle, and it illustrated the importance of the Middle East to the European powers.

The impending war, and the break up of the Ottoman Empire were foreshadowed in these conflicting interests. With Britain (allied with France and Russia) already a key opponent, and Germany supporting the Ottoman side, the Young Turk government had no choice but to enter the war alongside the Central powers.

The Creation of the Modern Middle East

As soon as the Ottoman Empire entered the war, Britain officially installed its protectorate in Egypt. The

Sultan then called for a *jihad* against the Allies, but found little support. After the failure of the Dardanelles offensive, which was aimed at preparing for a direct assault on Istanbul, the British tried to set up an internal front against the Turks by inciting the Arab provinces to revolt. Contacts were then made with Hussein, an Ottoman minister who was the head of the Hashemite family and the Sharif of Mecca. As the guardian of the holy places and as a descendant of the Prophet his moral authority was potentially considerable. Britain hoped to gain both his support and the benevolent neutrality of 100 million Indian Muslims. Negotiations began from Cairo under the aegis of the English High Commissioner McMahon: propositions and counter propositions which tried to delimit spheres of influence, and post-war frontiers became the subject of a famous correspondence, which was full of ambiguities, and later, denials. Hussein wanted to build a great "Arab Kingdom"; Faisal, one of his sons, was to mount the throne of Syria and Iraq, and Damascus would become the capital. Abdallah was to become King of Palestine, while Hussein would himself become King of Hijaz, and would re-establish the Arab caliphate for his own benefit. With some reservations the English government backed Hussein's plans. In 1916, with the help of Colonel Lawrence, the Arab revolt against the Turks was launched.

But Britain also had to nurture French interests in the region as France was its principal ally. This explains the Sykes-Picot agreement which was passed secretly just as the Arab revolt began. As well as "Greater Syria" (Syria, Lebanon and Palestine) the initial French claims included Silicia and Ottoman Kurdistan which surrounded the oil-producing region of Mosul. The negotiations did not take into account the plan for an Arab kingdom, which due to a subtle distinction between "direct possession" and "spheres of influence" was eventually placed under Arab suzerainty, meaning nominal Arab independence under French or British control.

The status of Palestine, including what is now Israel, Palestine and Jordan, which both powers wanted resolved – the third French Secular Republic remained faithful to its role as a protector of Christianity – was provisionally settled by a division of power between Britain

LAWRENCE OF ARABIA

Colonel T. E. Lawrence's life illustrated the paradoxes of secret diplomacy. He became known as Lawrence of Arabia because he was charged by the Foreign Office with negotiating with Hussein, Sharif of Mecca. He became the confidant of Hussein's son Faisal and took part in the Arab Revolt against Turkish domination in May 1916, where he was covered in glory on the battlefield. At the European peace conferences "the uncrowned King of the Arabs" fought his "final battle" in support of the promised "Arab Kingdom." He fought in vain; in the division of spoils from the Ottoman Empire there was no place for an Arab Kingdom. Conscious of his share of responsibility, albeit unintentional, for the treachery of his government Lawrence decided to disappear. Under a pseudonym he enrolled as an ordinary airman in the Royal Air Force. He died in a routine motorbike accident in 1935 far from the country and people of Arabia whom he had loved so much. ■

Ph. © Collection Violiet

and an international administration from the holy places. That would include all the powers with interests based on the Capitulation arrangements: France and Italy (Catholics); Great Britain (Protestants), Russia (Orthodox), etc.

For the British this provisional formula seemed a mere stop-gap. The British decided to play the Zionist card, for they were keen to gain the support of the more pro-German Jewish communities, and of those who supported the revolutionary process which was then taking place in Russia. What is more, the creation of a Jewish homeland and the probable conflicts between Zionists and Arabs in Palestine would facilitate British divide-and-rule strategies aimed at both the Zionist forces and the local Arab population, and would thus secure access to the Suez Canal. It was in this context, following difficult negotiations, that the famous Balfour Declaration was made. This was actually a letter addressed to Lord Rothschild, as a representative of the political committee of the Zionist organization, by the Foreign Secretary. Dated November 2, 1917 it announced that "His Majesty's Government view with favor the establishment in Pales-

*In March 1917 at the end of World War I, the entry of British troops into Baghdad was of strategic importance. The oil-producing region of Mosul which had been ceded to France in the Sykes-Picot Accord finally fell into British hands, and the modern Middle East took shape.
Ph © L'Illustration/Sygma*

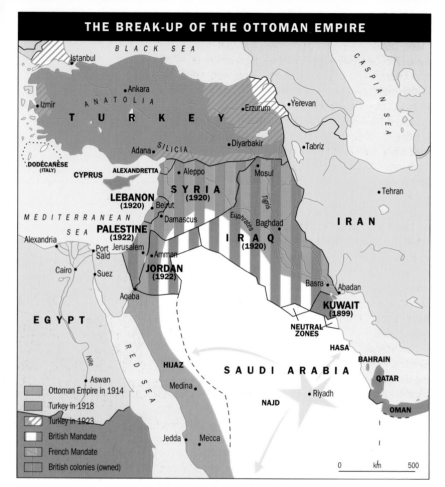

THE BREAK-UP OF THE OTTOMAN EMPIRE

Legend:
- Ottoman Empire in 1914
- Turkey in 1918
- Turkey in 1923
- British Mandate
- French Mandate
- British colonies (owned)

0   km   500

After the war the mandated powers decided on the frontiers. Greater Lebanon was created at the expense of Syria, which was itself divided into the Alawite States of Jebel Druze, Aleppo and Damascus. In 1939 the Sandjak of Alexandrette, which had a diverse population, was ceded by France to Turkey, with total disregard for international law.

tine of a national home for the Jewish people... it being clearly understood that nothing shall be done which may prejudice the civil and religious rights of existing non-Jewish communities in Palestine." Neither the status or the extent of this homeland were precisely determined, and the British never acknowledged the contradiction between Balfour and the promises of the Hussein-McMahon White Paper for Arab independence.

The Hussein-McMahon correspondence, the Sykes-Picot Agreement, and the Balfour Declaration were the three main, somewhat contradictory, documents that related to the break up of the Ottoman Empire. After the October Russian revolution the new Bolshevik leaders made public all secret agreements, most notably the Sykes-Picot Agreement. The vital importance of oil, which had been so clearly shown during the war, refocused British political direction. Britain wanted to control all the oil-producing areas in Persia and Mesopotamia. So they attacked Mosul with the barely concealed purpose of ousting the French. The French had to make the best of this: while they kept Syria and Lebanon, the rest of their "sphere of influence" returned to the Arabs — that is to say, to the English, as specified in the Sykes-Picot Agreement.

This new partition which was ratified at the beginning of 1919 was the origin of the border that today separates Syria and Iraq. The League of Nations passed a mandate that legalized the situation: the regime was to be temporary and was only to last until the countries were capable of governing themselves. All of the League of Nations mandates in the Middle East were supposed to be aimed at the ultimate independence of the new Arab states.

Further north, the Turkish nationalist movement led by General Mustafa Kemal, put an end to the plan of dividing the Anatolian plateau between the victorious powers (France, Great Britain, Italy and Greece) as they became know after the Treaty of Sèvres (August 10, 1920). The cease-fire at the end of the war led to an armistice and a revision of treaties in favor of Turkish national aspirations. In the meantime, more than one million Armenians – about half the population living in the Ottoman Empire – had perished in the massacres ordered by the government of the Young Turks in 1915. At the war's end, an Armenian Republic was proclaimed on the ashes of this genocide. But after the US Senate rejected President Wilson's proposal to place it under the protection of a US mandate, and despite it supposedly being under League of Nations protection, the new republic was left to its sad fate.

By giving his support to the establishment of a Jewish homeland in Palestine, Lord Balfour, the British Foreign Secretary, gave international recognition to the Zionist project.
Ph © Roger-Viollet

The Mosul agreement put an end to the plan for an Arab Kingdom as Britain was no longer invested in opposing the establishment of a French mandate in Syria. The French planned to pipe Iraqi oil across this region, in direct contradiction to promises made to Hussein and his son Faisal. Following the French ultimatum

Faisal's troops were defeated at the battle of Maysalun on July 24, 1920. In September of the same year Lebanon came into being. Faisal was taken up by the British and placed at the head of the Kingdom of Iraq.

In Arabia, Hussein, who was still Sharif of Mecca, clashed with Ibn Saud, a direct descendant of the original Saud, who had championed the Wahhabite cause. The Imam of the Wahhabites had remained on the sidelines of the conflict and the Arab revolt. In 1918 he had 70,000 men at his disposal who were members of *Ikhwan*, a politico-military fraternity driven by a strong religious fervor.

While Hussein concentrated all his ambitions on the Fertile Crescent, Ibn Saud concentrated on his plans to reunify the Arab peninsula. The two men, who were very different, hated each other. Ibn Saud did not mind confirming that he "hated Hussein more than any man on earth. As for his sons, Ali, Abdallah and Faisal, I would like to crush them with my heel like a nest of scorpions." This rivalry passed down from generation to generation and even accounts for some differences today. In 1924 Ibn Saud was finally able to put his plan into action. When, after the abolition of the Turkish caliphate Hussein declared himself Caliph, the Wahhabites denounced him as an impostor and attacked

IBN SAUD AND THE HOLY PLACES OF ISLAM

Once he had conquered Mecca, Ibn Saud called a pan-Islamic congress in 1926 which entrusted him with the administration of the holy places of Islam.

"Suddenly at the instigation of an Afghan delegate the congressmen added an item on the independence of the holy places to the agenda... As far as Ibn Saud was concerned, he was the conqueror and ruler of Hijaz, and it was up to him to administer them... On entering the hall he was taken violently aside by a delegate:... 'What right do you have to be King?' Ibn Saud thought this was going too far. He drew himself up to his full height and he looked the Congress up and down:

'Which of you,' he asked in a thunderous voice, 'could guarantee the safety of the holy places against any foreign interference?'

The delegates exchanged embarrassed glances and buried their noses in their papers.

'I repeat my question. Which of you could guarantee the safety of the holy places against any foreign interference?'

As nobody replied he continued:

'I alone here am free! So I alone can do so,' declared Ibn Saud in a tone that brooked no opposition. 'Take this independence as fact and let's talk about it no more!'

This peremptory intervention closed the Assembly's debate." ■

Benoist-Méchin. *The Wolf and the Leopard: Ibn Saud or the Birth of a Kingdom.* Albin Michel, 1975. 281.

Hijaz. This time the British did not stop him, as the old Sharif was no longer of any use to them. Hussein had to flee. Ibn Saud declared himself King of Najd and Hijaz and in 1926 a pan-Islamic congress entrusted him with the administration of the holy places. The decision to do so was not unanimous and would lead to further conflict.

The new Middle Eastern states which came into being at the end of the First World War were to have a difficult time; their delimitation was mainly driven by foreign interests and the partitions were arbitrary. The only exceptions were the Iraqi-Iranian borders, which were more or less stabilized by the secular struggles between Persia and the Sublime Porte, the Egyptian border with Sinai, and the rather special case of Saudi Arabia. Basically, the twentieth century Middle East is a Franco-British creation which took little notice of the region's own dynamics. The victorious powers of the Great War set up precarious structures in a troubled geopolitical region.

As in Europe, where the Treaty of Versailles, with the problem of reparations and the Danzig Corridor had held the seeds of conflict of the Second World War, post-war arbitrations had led to a "new Middle Eastern Question." This question, which led to many of today's problems, has still not been resolved.

United in their faith the Ikhwan ("the Brothers") were the key players in the Saudi conquest. But their rejection of new borders threatened the post-war mandated order. Under pressure from the British, Ibn Saud crushed the rebel fighters at the battle of Sibila in 1929.
Ph © René Burri/Magnum

Chapter 2

OPPOSING
VIEWS

THE POST-WAR MIDDLE EAST, NO LONGER PART OF THE OTTOMAN EMPIRE, BUT DOMINATED BY AN ALL POWERFUL WEST, WAS IN SEARCH OF ITS OWN POLITICAL AGENDA. THE PROBLEM WAS: WHICH AGENDA?

The vicissitudes of the end of World War I and the break-up of the Ottoman Empire, and most particularly, Turkey's change of political direction, made a return to the old regime unthinkable. Under the direction of Mustapha Kemal, Turkey had successfully insisted on a revision of the Treaty of Sèvres, expelled the Greeks, and set up a republic. Once the Caliphate was abolished in 1924, Turkey turned its back on its Eastern past and started on a path to authoritarian modernism; the Roman alphabet was soon adopted, and the wearing of beards and veils forbidden. The impact of this was considerable: after all, the main symbol of Muslim unity was disappearing. Surrounded by Turkey and Persia, who both enjoyed a certain stability and a relative independence, the Arab Middle East, dominated by France and Great Britain, was left stranded without an alternative agenda to oppose the West, and without a real understanding of current events.

Even earlier in the nineteenth century the Ottoman Empire had been confronted by a triumphant industrial civilization, a Western world which revelled in its new technology. It seemed that the Ottoman Empire had failed and many thought that an "authentic" solution to this apparent failure would be to renew links with the past: the myth of the "Golden Age" dated from this time, and it mattered little whether this age was Muslim, Pharaonic,

*Oil was a great "shock" to the people of the Middle East, long before it rocked the West's economy in 1973 because it accentuated the imbalances which in many cases had come about at the beginning of the century. Nevertheless, the traditional way of life carried on. The faithful's prayers were directed to Mecca, and religion was, very often, one of the only landmarks in an unstable world.
Ph © Marc Riboud/Magnum*

Modern Turkey owes a debt to Mustapha Kemal (1881–1938) who realized that he had to oppose the post-war divisions. The Treaty of Sèvres in August 1920 took the richest territories from the Aegean coast, as well as the Kurd and Armenian republics, and gave them to the Greeks, the Italians and the French. One year later the Turkish national uprising led to a decisive military victory over the Greeks, and a revision of treaties in favor of Turkey.
Ph © Collection Viollet

Hittite or whatever. For everybody concerned the meeting of East and West proved to be something of a challenge – a challenge that still exists today. It is no exaggeration to say that Islam, particularly that of the Muslim Brothers, is a modernist movement. Islam, like all religions, is also a social and historical phenomenon, with limitless potential, and capable of many forms of expression.

Islam and Reformism

In the face of Western pressure the first reforms of the Ottoman and Muslim civilization took place quite naturally. One of the first major objectives was to show Europe that Islam was not an obstacle to progress, and that the religion was itself capable of reform and could show the way forward. An equal objective was to restore an Islamic civilization which was capable of resisting European aggression. Jamal ad-Din al-Afhani (1838–1897) and Mohammad 'Abduh (1849–1905) dominated this period, and as they were faced with a decadence which they considered essentially spiritual, they sought to find the true path of Islam once more. Rather than submit to foreign domination, the Muslims decided to draw on their past and turn their temporary weakness into strength.

The founding movement of political Islam, the Muslim Brothers, came about as a direct result of the reformist problem. But in the Egypt of 1928 the historical context had altered radically. Like his predecessors, Hassan al-Banna, the founder and first Supreme Guide of the Brotherhood, saw that the basis of Islamic reform lay in the application of the *Shari'a*, and in the maintenance of the Caliphate. In 1928 Western influence was spreading and the Caliphate had just been abolished. Saad Zaghlul's Wafd party was at the forefront of the political scene, and was supported by an Egyptian nationalist movement that was essentially secular in nature, and respected the rules of European parliamentary government. For al-Banna, this historical moment was not so much a time for renewal as a time to defend a civilization which he saw as being under-

These tenets were laid down when the movement began in 1928 and still hold good.

1. I believe that everything is under God's Command; that Mohammad is the seal of all prophecy addressed to all men, that (Eternal) Retribution is a reality, that the Qur'an is the Book of God, that Islam is a complete law that leads us in this life and the next. And I promise to recite to myself (each day) a passage from the Qur'an, to keep to the authentic Tradition, to study the life of the Prophet, and the history of his followers.

2. I believe that correct action, virtue and knowledge are among the pillars of Islam. And I promise to act correctly in carrying out the religious practices and in avoiding evil doings. I pledge myself to good habits, and I will abhor bad habits, I will disseminate Muslim customs as widely as possible, I will choose love and attachment over rivalry and condemnation, I will not take recourse to tribunals unless I have to, I will reinforce the customs and language of Islam, and I will work to disseminate science and useful knowledge in all sections of the nation...

4. I believe that the Muslim is responsible for his family, that he has a duty to keep it in good health, in the faith, and in good habits. And I promise to do my best to inculcate the teachings of Islam in my family. I will not place my sons in a school which will not uphold their beliefs, and their good habits. I will not allow them any magazines, books or publications which deny the teachings of Islam, and equally organizations, groups or clubs of this kind.

5. I believe that the Muslim has the right to bring Islam to life by the renaissance of its various peoples, and that the banner of Islam should cover mankind, and that each Muslim should educate the world in Muslim principles. And I promise to fight to achieve this aim as long as I live, and to sacrifice everything I have to this end. ■

***I**n August 1990 demonstrators linked to the Jordanian Muslim Brotherhood massed in the streets of Amman to denounce the "unholy" presence of the American army in the sacred land of Saudi Arabia.*
Ph. © D.Erwitt/Magnum

Wafd, the great Egyptian nationalist party, founded in 1919 by Saad Zaghlul, managed to unite Copts and Muslims in the struggle against the British occupier. As well as placards which showed victims of the repression, one in this demonstration implored "The spirits of our martyrs beseech you: avenge them!"
Ph © Keystone

mined from within. The example of Kemal's secularist Turkey had proved to him that the adoption of Western values, even for patriotic ends, could only lead to subservience and atheism. Al-Banna thought that the struggle against foreign invasion, which he compared with a renewed struggle against the Crusaders, should be paramount. To counter this invasion, he established the supreme constitutional system of Islam which was designed to encompass all human activity.

The Muslim Brothers devised a program of action based on the teachings of the Qur'an. Now that the Caliphate had been abolished, the Brothers wanted to gather all believers together and rebuild the *Umma* (community of Muslims) under their protection. They considered themselves to be the only true inheritors of Sunni philosophy, but at the same time the movement sought to encompass "the Salafite sense of purpose, Sufi spirituality, and the political and communal system of Islam, which encompassed a social philosophy and an economic order." It was clear that by focusing on traditionalism the Muslim Brothers wanted to hold a monopoly on Islamic fundamentalism.

The Brotherhood's claim to be the sole incarnation of the Islamic legacy soon provoked opposition, because the Brothers were not only opposed to Westernization, but also to the institutional Islam of al-Azhar and to Sufi mysticism, which they considered to be riddled with superstition. They also opposed the descendants of the first reformers, of whom Sheikh Ali Abd al-Razzaq was one of the most distinguished. In his work entitled *Islam and the Foundation of Power,* published in 1925, he tried to demonstrate, with the help of passages from the Qur'an, the essentially spiritual nature of the Revelation. He felt that since the Caliphate was not mentioned in the text of the Qur'an, politics and religion should remain separate. In the post-war context his work caused a scandal, and the liberal voice of Islam, caught between an essentially Western secularism and the fundamentalist preachings of the Brothers, was subdued.

The Muslim Brotherhood

After the abolition of the Caliphate, the Muslim Brotherhood's version of political Islam initially triumphed. Their movement, which could be called "neo-Islam" – as it had come about from an unprecedented historical situation – became the depository of all legitimacy and authenticity. Helped by both a simple and decisive program and by the circumstances of the time, the movement saw rapid growth. Branches sprang up in Sudan, Jordan, and Syria. The initial success of the movement was due to mobilization techniques which foreshadowed those of the twentieth century; it resorted to mass militantism, adopted a strictly hierarchical structure, and its believers followed a military path subscribing to the doctrine of *jihad*.

*W*hen the young King Farouk ascended the throne in 1936 he benefited from a wave of popular sympathy that he was soon to squander. Deposed by Nasser's agents on July 26, 1952 he went into exile on board his yacht.
Ph © Harlingue/Viollet

Despite all the politcal upheavals and the ideological struggles which have divided the Middle East for the best part of a century, daily life has remained unchanged for most of the population. In the villages the women prepare the khobz, *a large round loaf and a staple food, in the traditional ovens.*
Ph © Cartier-Bresson/Magnum

Al-Banna declared: "The first stage of Holy War is to rid your own heart of evil; the ultimate stage is armed struggle for the sake of God. Intermediate stages are fighting by means of the spoken word, the pen, the hand, and the word of truth which must be addressed to any unjust authority. Our apostolic movement can only thrive through combat." As they had a long-term strategy of penetrating the social fabric, the Brothers established a network of centers of education and mutual support. Once the Wafd had been discredited, the Muslim Brotherhood became the leading Egyptian mass movement. At the beginning of the fifties they had approximately two million members, because they had benefited from the emotion provoked by the Palestinian struggle and from the corruption evident in Egyptian political life.

The debate over political Islam provided a good illustration of the tensions which ran through Eastern society, and the ideological consequences of foreign occupation. "Modernism" came to be associated with the West, so "fundamentalism," although difficult to define, became more appealing.

There was a tendency to dwell on an idealized vision of past glories, and the two camps of modernism and fundamentalism became engaged in a debate that was more likely to lead to conflict than to resolution.

In actual terms contemporary Islam was to oscillate between integration with the political system, in order to bring about reform, and non-integration, because of its capacity for violence. The Brothers' activism led to disturbances. In the forties certain special units who were fighting in Palestine refused to rally with the official army, despite being commanded to do so by Hassan al-Banna. There were riots and violent demonstrations. The Supreme Guide lost control of a section of his troops, and in 1948 the movement was dissolved by royal decree. Caught up in a spiral of violence and repression, Hassan al-Banna was assassinated on February 12, 1949, almost certainly by the police. He became the martyr of a cause which was to undergo yet further radicalism (see Chapter Six).

ARAB NATIONALISM FIRST

"**A**rab nationalism is not confined to the inhabitants of the Arab Peninsula any more than it is specifically for Muslims. Quite on the contrary it includes all those who belong to the Arab countries, and who speak Arabic, whether they are Egyptian, Kuwaiti, Moroccans, Muslims or Christians, Sunni, Shiites or Druze, Catholics, Orthodox or Protestants. Anybody can be a child of Arab nationalism provided that they ally themselves to an Arab country, and speak the Arabic language... The differences and divergences that one now sees between the Arab states – from the point of view of their legislative, economic and administrative structures, and in their political orientation – are all the result of years of occupation. They are the fruits of imperialism; they are both recent and contingent. Arabs are one *umma*.

...Now that it has woken from its long sleep, Arab nationalism exudes vitality. There is absolutely no question of a glorious past, but of a starting point to a glorious future which will see the establishment of a 'unified Arab State' as well as the progress of the 'reborn Arab *umma*' toward the highest peaks of science and civilization." ■

S. Al-Housaril (1880–1969), one of the first theoreticians of Arab nationalism, quoted by A. Abdelmalek. *Contemporary Arab Political Thought.* Le Seuil. 1971.

The Idea of an Arab Nation

Political Islam was only one of the many responses to the decadence which had resulted from the dismemberment of the Ottoman Empire. Eager to inspire an "Arab Renaissance" a group of intellectuals and men of letters determined to dust off the Arab culture and language, and make it into an instrument of communication and progress; here

again they were going back to their roots. They designed the press, and helped to disseminate a modern language which was a combination of classical Arabic, which had never been easily accessible, and the various dialects. The confirmation of their Arab nationality helped these men of the *nahda,* most frequently of Syrian or Lebanese extraction, although sometimes Christian, to resist Ottoman, or rather Muslim, domination. This in turn led to the new ambiguities which were apparent in the beginnings of the pan-Arabic movement.

For thousands of years Egyptians have gathered together along the Nile valley. At the beginning of spring, Jews, Christians and Muslims celebrate Sham an-Naseem by cutting down palm branches and gathering on the river banks. This ancient rite, of Pharaonic origin, is still celebrated today.
Ph © Harlingue/Viollet

Pan-Arabism was even more of a contemporary creation than political Islam. As we have seen, Arab nationalism came into being in the seventh century in the cradle of Islam which had united all the scattered tribes of the desert peninsula in a common project. Contemporary Arab nationalism, which found its clearest expression in the works of Michel 'Aflaq (1910–1989) the founder of the *Ba'ath* movement, was fundamentally utopic. Taking a stand against the post-war divisions, 'Aflaq advocated the concept of an Arab nation, at the very time when circumstances made its realization more difficult than ever. For the ideologues of Arab nationalism, Islam was a cultural heritage, an essential and inseparable element of Arab national history, for after all God had revealed the Qur'an in Arabic. Such a movement was truly revolutionary in Islamic lands, for it made it possible to reunify and reinvigorate all the Arabic parts of the Ottoman Empire.

This concept led to an ambiguous relationship between Islam and Arab nationalism as there was conflict over whether religion or the fatherland was more important. For the followers of political Islam, the universal message of Islam did not recognize national ties, which it considered mere idolatrous chauvinism; it could not understand the Western concept of the homeland.

In reality the relationship between Islam and Arab nationalism was more complex; the latter was only gradually (and never quite entirely) freed from its Islamic points of reference. This sometimes resulted in paradoxical situations. For example, in 1892 a dispute arose between the British authorities and the Ottomans over the ownership of the Taba territory in Sinai. The budding Egyptian nationalist movement came out in favor of the Sultan rather than Egypt. Similarly the "Arab Revolt" which Sharif Hussein launched in 1916 found its justification from the call to *jihad* by a religious dignitary opposing an impious chauvinistic Turkish government. Arab nationalism took time to make its mark. Pan-Arabism was further complicated by old rivalries which were interwoven with dynastic interests. The most important question was the location of the center of the Arab nation. There was no shortage of contenders. As we have

Political Islam developed alongside Western domination; became violent alongside it, and will only lose its strength alongside it.

Tarik al-Bishri

seen, the idea developed in the Syrian and Lebanese provinces; they were proud of their Umayyad past and they had been affected both by the Ottoman rule and the post-war divisions. In Iraq, Faisal had always dreamed of the great Arab Kingdom which had been promised to his father by the British. But in Saudi Arabia, his rival Ibn Saud, proud of his new title of Guardian of the holy places, and soon rich from the blessing of oil, wanted to play a dominant role. Egypt, because of its sheer size and demographic weight, as well as its position halfway between the Arab East and the Maghreb also wanted to join in Mehmet Ali's plan. But Egypt was soon occupied and separated from the Empire and started to become industrialized along Western lines. A modern bourgeoisie appeared. In 1919 they rallied the Egyptian people around the Wafd, a party which was steadily developing an Egyptian nationalism with Pharaonic overtones. What, for example, did these men have in common with the old-fashioned Wahhabism of an Ibn Saud? At the same time, Egypt's advances down the paths of independence and modernization helped the Muslim Brothers' rebellion; in short, historical differences and disparate political, social and economic situations thwarted any attempts at unity. At the beginning of the twentieth century the Egyptian Saad Zaghlul had expressed his views on the hopelessness of any plans for unification: "Add zero and zero and the answer will always be zero!" It was only in the forties that the idea of an Arab nation, which ranged from the Gulf to the Atlantic, really took hold.

The Affirmation of the Minorities

The intervention of European powers in the internal politics of individual countries only served to complicate further an already tortuous state of regional affairs. The national struggles reinforced the divergences and differences of understanding between the various countries in the region. This was how King Faisal, who had been expelled from Syria by the French, and then "recuperated" by the English in Iraq, came to enjoy a rather mixed posterity: he

SUNNISM AND SHI'ISM

Shi'ism appeared at the very beginning of Islamic history: it came about from the political problems posed by the Prophet's succession. The Prophet, who died in 632, had not left any precise instructions on this matter, and the supporters of his son-in-law Ali, thought that his qualities, together with his family ties to Mohammad, best qualified him for the Caliphate. Finding an egalitarian Islam, which was against the demonstration of any tribal or ethnic ties, still very evocative, Ali crystallized the opposition. After his assassination in 661 his followers developed a legitimist understanding of the Caliphate and chose their own Imams from among Ali's descendants. Shi'ism, which initially grouped together all opponents of the established order, thus founded a tradition of religious opposition to political power. The "acquisition of goodness and the expulsion of evil"

prescribed in the Qur'an, in effect authorized revolt against an unjust power. One of the common traits in the various Shi'ite sects is the belief in a "hidden Imam" who will reappear at the end of time and establish a reign of justice. In Shi'ism – unlike Sunnism – the existence and the role of the clergy is very important as they are charged with interpreting doctrine and training the community. Shi'ism has many branches (see table below) which are mainly concerned with the legitimacy and number of the Imam who are descended from Ali. The main branch, which holds sway in Iran, recognizes twelve Imams. Certain sects, such as the Druze and Alawites, who believe in the divinity of Ali and the transmigration of souls, have developed esoteric doctrines which have put them very much on the fringes of traditional belief. The Yezidis provide an extreme example; wrongly called devil

worshippers, they have been constantly persecuted right up to the present day. Some tens of thousands of Yezidis still live a secluded existence today in the north of Iraq. Because of a desire to protect the unity of the *umma* and because of the lack of an interpretative authority which would be considered capable of settling Islamic conflicts, the diverse Shi'ite sects are only rarely excluded from the community of believers. Persecutions normally result from the need to quell disorder. Faced with the Shi'ite movement, Sunnism defined itself differently: it gathered all its believers around the Sunna – the whole of the Qur'anic tradition and the *hadiths* or sayings of the Prophet – and did not develop a separate doctrine. According to tradition, Mohammad predicted that his followers would divide into 99 sects of which only one would be saved. ∎

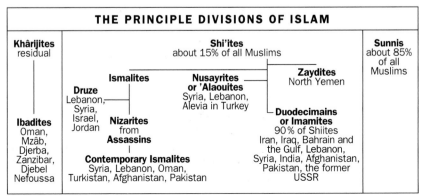

THE PRINCIPLE DIVISIONS OF ISLAM

Khârijites residual			Shi'ites about 15% of all Muslims			Sunnis about 85% of all Muslims
		Ismalites	**Nusayrites or 'Alaouites** Syria, Lebanon, Alevia in Turkey	**Zaydites** North Yemen		
	Druze Lebanon, Syria,					
Ibadites Oman, Mzâb, Djerba, Zanzibar, Djebel Nefoussa	Israel, Jordan	**Nizarites** from **Assassins** | **Contemporary Ismalites** Syria, Lebanon, Oman, Turkistan, Afghanistan, Pakistan		**Duodecimains or Imamites** 90% of Shiites Iran, Iraq, Bahrain and the Gulf, Lebanon, Syria, India, Afghanistan, Pakistan, the former USSR		

was glorified in Syria as a hero of the nationalist struggle, but was considered by the Iraqis to be an English lackey. As for Egypt, one of its first national-istic claims concerned the "unity of the Nile Valley." The subtext of this slogan was a desire to annex the Sudan: in its struggle against colonialism, Egypt was itself to become a colonizer.

In 1919 a General Syrian Congress solemnly affirmed its attachment to the idea of a Greater Syria, in total opposition to the plans of the Ver-sailles conference to divide British and French con-

The Saudi monarch's visit to Cairo in 1952. Despite political differences, the alliance between Riyadh and Cairo is a geopolitical constant which looks to counterbalance the strength of the Fertile Crescent, and primarily Iraq, in the heart of the Arab Middle East.
Ph © Keystone

trol of the region, separate Syria and Lebanon, and confirm the terms of the Sykes-Picot Agreement. In fact, the pretensions of the Syrian delegates relied on a socio-cultural unity which had long been recog-nized in the "land of Sham." This Syrian irreden-tism, which had been clearly expressed by the Congress, gives an essential key to the understand-ing of contemporary conflicts. This feeling went on to manifest itself in the Syrian Nationalist Party founded in 1932 by Antun Sa'adé. For Sa'adé, whose party had decidedly fascist tendencies, Arab nationalism was not just a linguistic notion with religious overtones, but the Syrian nation was the fruit of a long historical genesis which found its beginnings, and its "natural" expansionist inclinations, in Ancient Assyria. He was not afraid of laying claim to Silicia, Sinai, and Cyprus, as well as the entire Fertile Crescent – all of which had been ruled from the eighth to the sixth centuries BC by the Assyrians.

The mandatory powers exploited the ideological confusion and the diversity in the region and oper-

TOWARD A GREATER SYRIA

Resolution of the Syrian General Congress, Damascus July 2, 1919

We, the undersigned, members of the Syrian General Congress, assembled in Damascus on July 2, 1919, elected representatives of the Muslim, Christian and Jewish inhabitants of our respective districts [have adopted] the following resolutions:

1. We request total political independence for Syria within the following borders [there follows a delimitation roughly corresponding to Syrian territories, south-west Turkey, Libya, Palestine and Jordan].

2. We request the establishment of a constitutional monarchy in Syria... and we hope that the Emir Faisal, who has worked so hard for our liberation, and enjoys our full confidence, will become our King.

3. Taking into consideration that the Arabs of Syria are no less capable than the people of other nations (such as the Bulgarians, the Greeks, or the Rumanians) of exercising their independence, we protest against Article XXIII of the Constitution of the League of Nations, which relegates us to the rank of an inferior nation, which needs to be put under the tutelage of a mandatory power...

6. We do not recognize that the French government has any rights in Syria, and we reject all French proposals to offer us assistance, or to exercise their authority on any part of our territory.

7. We reject the claims of the Zionists who are trying to establish a national homeland in the southern part of Syria known as Palestine, and we are opposed to any Jewish migration in our country. We do not recognize any cogency in their arguments, and we consider that their claims represent a grave threat to our national political and economic life. Our Jewish compatriots will continue to enjoy their rights, and will continue to participate in the exercising of our communal responsibilities.

8. We are opposed to any dismemberment of Syria and we refuse to allow the separation of Palestine, or the coastal region of West Lebanon from the Mother Country...

10. ...We dare to hope that the Peace Conference will recognize that we would not have rebelled against the Turks, under whose government we enjoyed political and civil privileges, as well as the right of representation, if the Turks had not refused us the right of a national existence... ∎

Antonius G. *The Arab Awakening.* New York: Paragon Books, 1979. 440–442.

ated using the tactic of divide and rule. This policy helped to undermine the principles of co-existence, which had characterized the Ottoman Empire at its peak, and to exacerbate the structural weaknesses which had been inherited from that same regime. France and Great Britain managed both to reinforce the differences between peoples and movements and to nourish dreams of unity be they pan-Islamic, pan-Arab or Syrian.

In this respect France's work in Syria was revealing. After its military victory at Maysalun in 1920, the French mandate divided the country into four states: the Alawites in northern Syria, the Djebel Druze, Aleppo, and Damascus. In granting autonomy to the Druze and the Alawite communities France helped to undermine the legitimacy of the nation state that it was supposed to be establishing. Furthermore it brought the problem of minorities back into prominence; they now had to struggle for political control of a territory or a state. So in 1924, encouraged by France, the Alawite leaders left the Syrian federation and declared themselves an independent state. Despite a later return to the Syrian fold the Alawite attitude had revived the old suspicions which the majority of Muslims had held about them.

At the same time relations between Christians

and Muslims took a new direction. The protection of Christian minorities by means of the Capitulations was a traditional means of influence which was largely favorable to Europe. The Western powers propounded their "civilizing" message through their missions and their schools, and they set themselves up as intermediaries between religious groups.

At the beginning of the century, in the heart of the Ottoman Empire, France had successfully set up a network of primary schools which had educated nearly 100,000 pupils. More than two-thirds of these children were Christian, although actually two-thirds of the general population held other beliefs. With the blessing of the Western powers, minorities were able to reaffirm their identities: so the Copts reconfirmed their belief that they were the only Egyptians from pure Pharaonic stock, the Iraqi Nestorians were the only true Assyrians, and even the Lebanese Maronites were the only true Phoenicians. As a result the national governments mistrusted all their claims or even any sectarian utterances.

The case of the Assyrians was a tragic example. This small community of orthodox Christians, who had regrouped in the mountainous region of Hakkâri on the Turkish-Iranian border, had extracted from Britain the formal promise of a future national

In Lebanon the French High Commissioner relied on the leaders of various communities while still stressing the importance of the traditional links with the Maronites. In 1926 a Lebanese constitution was issued. For General Weygand, the High Commissioner in Beirut (in the center of the photograph) it was the "[French] constitution, decked with bougainvillea and wearing a keffiyeh on its head." Ph © L'Illustration/Sygma

homeland in return for their support in the First World War. Believing in this commitment, the Assyrians played the British card exclusively after the war; in the supplementary corps of the Iraqi "Levies" they helped suppress various Shi'ite, Arab or Kurdish revolts. But when Hakkâri was given to Turkey in 1925 their hopes evaporated and in 1932 their uprising was crushed – with the help of the British.

In Lebanon in 1936 leading villagers expound demands such as permission to grow tobacco and the opening of new schools to President Emile Eddé.
Ph © Keystone

Without the constant support of the Western powers, the divisions among the heterogeneous populations who lived in the same territory prevented the formation of new sovereign states based on a unified community. With the evaporation of their post-war dreams some minorities were seduced by the secular and egalitarian rhetoric of Arab nationalism, in the same way other minorities were to contribute to the birth of the communist parties. It is worth noting the steady progress of a middle class of administrators whose social rise was directly attributable to the values of the modern state. This was particularly true of the Army's Officer Corps, who, after 1945, were to play a fundamental role in many countries in the region.

The Problem of Democracy

Democracy in the liberal and parliamentary sense of the word developed in the West in the nineteenth century: it had no traditional or cultural references in the East, and it was "imported" at the same time as the League of Nations' mandates. Between the wars, parliamentary government, especially in Egypt, was viewed as an instrument wielded by foreign oppressors intent on exacerbating the differences of opinion and the tensions inherited from the Ottoman order. But the tense state of the world in the thirties also had important repercussions in the Middle East, where some political parties were influenced

by the rise of Fascism in Europe: besides the Syrian Nationalist Party of Antun Sa'adé, there were the Phalangists founded by Pierre Gemayel in Lebanon, the Green Shirts, the "Islamic nationalists" from the Young Egypt movement, and the Futuwwa in Iraq who were inspired by the Hitler Youth Movement. These new movements exacerbated old divisions, while democracy still waited to happen.

This was the political and historical background at the end of the nineteenth century until the period between the two world wars. The muddied conflicts of the rest of the twentieth century would find their roots and their own logic here. Zionism, which came into the fray burdened with serious liabilities and which provided new reasons for conflict, would only aggravate the structural tensions of the region.

Strongly impressed by the Hitler model, Pierre Geymayal, a young chemist from Beirut, founded the Kataeb Party, or the Phalangists. They enrolled many young people in their movement and aggressively demanded a permanent Greater Lebanon which would enshrine Maronite community values. The political importance of the Phalangists was limited until the 1975 war.
Ph © Keystone

Chapter 3

NEXT YEAR IN
JERUSALEM

ISRAEL'S VERY EXISTENCE IN THE HEART OF THE MIDDLE EAST
POLARIZED MOST OF THE CONFLICTS IN THE REGION. IT IS REALLY
ONLY POSSIBLE TO UNDERSTAND THE PASSIONATE FEELINGS THAT
ISRAEL PROVOKED BY STUDYING THE HISTORY OF ZIONISM.

I srael enshrines the Zionist movement which worked to re-establish the political sovereignty of the Jewish people, and to return it to the land of its forefathers. It is rare for such a Utopian dream actually to come to fruition. The term "Zionism" came about in 1890, and refers to Zion, the hill in Jerusalem where the first Temple was built, and which came to symbolize the Promised Land. Zionism came about in response to European anti-Semitism and this has had a lasting effect on the movement. In fact, the State of Israel did not really set itself up against – or in spite of – the Palestinian Arabs, but against a West that had rejected the Jews. But because the driving force of Jewish immigration and its political and cultural references were European-based, Zionism was seen as foreign to the region and associated with colonialism.

The arrival of the first pioneers coincided with the break up of the Ottoman Empire and consolidation of European domination of the area. This influx was immediately perceived to be a result of foreign domination. In 1919, the Palestinian delegation to the Syrian Congress gave voice to this impression: "Zionism is more dangerous than the French occupation [in Syria] for they [the French] know that they are foreigners, while the Zionists think they are at home in Palestine..." The Jewish settlers and the Palestinian Arabs saw matters from different historical perspec-

*In 1947 the "Exodus," a boat which was carrying more than 4,000 refugees from the Holocaust, was turned back from the port of Haifa by British authorities who were keen to stop Jewish immigration to Palestine. This drama shook the Western world, which then looked favorably upon the creation of Israel.
Ph © Magnum*

The Temple of Solomon built in 10 BC bears witness to the power and the splendor of the ancient Kingdom of Israel. The sacred walls shelter the Holy of Holies, the center of the universe, the Tablets of the Law given to Moses by God on Mount Sinai. Only the chief priest can go in there once a year on Yom Kippur. According to tradition the Temple was destroyed by the Babylonians in 586 BC

magnificence of the building. Early in his prophecy Mohammad commanded his followers to turn their prayers toward Jerusalem. It was there, according to the Qur'an, that the prophet finished his mysterious nocturnal journey. In 687 AD, during the first century of the *hijra*, the Umayyad Caliph Abd al-Malik built on the foundations of the Haram al-Sharif Temple, which comprised the Dome of the Rock, and the al-Aqsa Mosque, at the supposed

because the Jewish people had failed to follow Moses' commandments. It was then rebuilt around 500 BC, renovated by Herod in the first century BC and then destroyed again in the rebellion against Rome in 70 AD. Only one section of the incredible Western Wall, the Wailing Wall, was left standing by Titus, and it shows the sheer

site of the prophet's ascension. While the Hebrew name for Jerusalem, *Yerushalaïm*, means "City of Peace," *Al-Quds* means "Holiness" in Arabic. After Mecca and Medina it is the third holy place of Islam. The Muslim religious authorities controlled Haram al-Sharif, and consequently access to the Wailing Wall, so the co-existence between the two

sanctuaries was problematic at times. However, in 1928 the Grand Mufti decided to make the sanctuary larger. This involved making an opening in the Wall. In the face of this provocation there were many clashes. In August 1929 a defense demonstration organized by the *Haganah* gave rise to a series of disturbances and murders. These incidents were the cause of the first widespread Arab revolt against the entire Palestinian mandate. When East Jerusalem was captured in 1967 "the liberation of the Wall" became a symbol of prime importance for all Israelis. Some believers hoped to see the building of the Third Temple, three thousand years after the reign of Solomon. For according to the prophet Zachariah "the feet of our Lord shall stand in that day upon the Mount of Olives which is before Jerusalem on the East; and the Mount of Olives shall cleave in the midst thereof toward the East and toward the West, and there shall be a very great valley, and half of the mountain shall remove toward the North and half of it toward the South" (Zachariah 14). Following this cataclysm the two mosques would disappear and then the Temple could be rebuilt. But anxious to hasten the advent of messianic times, some extremists wanted to destroy Haram al-Sharif... ∎

tives and their differences were aired in this country which was known to one side as Israel and the other as Palestine. The tragic and ambivalent paradox of Zionism is that it was seen as a plan for Jewish emancipation by the West, but as a colonial enterprise by the East. In short, for the people of the Middle East, conflict inevitably arose from the effective political and symbolic occupation of a land that was already inhabited.

The Origins of Zionism

It was in the nineteenth century, when justice and equality seemed impossible for all citizens, that the Zionists first planned to leave Europe and establish a Jewish homeland in Palestine. Disappointed with assimilation, Moses Hess (1812–1875), Léon Pinsker (1821–1891) and Theodor Herzl (1860–1904) became the founding fathers of the movement. Since individual emancipation had failed, they decided to work toward collective emancipation. They responded to criticism about the lack of a Jewish homeland by making known their desire to return to their ancestral home of Palestine. They talked of the the importance of working the land and of a new people and these ideals found expression in the *kibbutzim,* the collective communities which, from 1911 on became the backbone of the Zionist presence in Palestine.

As it happened, the plan for a Jewish homeland immediately met strong resistance within the Jewish world. For a long time Zionists remained a minority group, whose ideas were fiercely disputed because they insisted more on the nationalistic, rather than the religious, characteristics of Judaism. For the orthodox Jew, this secular enterprise was sacrilegious because it subordinated Jewish identity to a political project, and it aimed to build a nation before the coming of the Messiah. The great majority of Jews remained faithful to the idea of individual emancipation within their home countries, and accused the Zionists, who planned collective secession from the West, of playing the anti-Semitic game of calling on Jews to leave their homes. It was not until Hitler's

Built in 687 on the foundations of the Temple of Jerusalem, the Dome of the Rock, or the Omar Mosque, is one of the three holy places of Islam. It is there that the prophet completed his mysterious nocturnal journey: "Praise be to him who in the night, transported his servant from one holy shrine (Medina) to the furthest holy shrine (al-Aqsa) where we have blessed the surroundings in order to show him some of our marvelous symbols."
Sourate XVII. Sayings of the Children of Israel, p 50.
Ph. © L.L.-Viollet

persecutions – when the world looked on in silence – that Jews came to see Zionism as a viable last resort. In 1945 people the world over were appalled at the discovery of the death camps. From the Odessa pogroms of 1881 and from the horrors of Auschwitz, Zionism acquired a tragic legitimacy.

However, while European anti-Semitism lay the foundations of Israel's legitimacy, the Arabs thought the West was absolving itself of its guilty conscience cheaply, and at the expense of their own national rights, an abuse they would not allow.

The new Zionist immigrants, who were full of European ideals, ignored or minimized the difficulties of

coexistence with this native population: they were planning to colonize Palestine with new progressive, civilizing ideals. They adopted the slogan: "A land without a people for a people without a land!" and dreamed, according to Chaim Weizmann, of building "a Palestine as Jewish as England is English."

THEODOR HERZL AND THE ORIGINS OF ZIONISM

Theodor Herzl (1860 – 1904) "the harbinger of the State" is considered to be the founder of political Zionism; he is credited with giving the movement a structure and disseminating its beliefs. In 1895 this Viennese journalist, who was an assimilated Jew and an admirer of Enlightenment France, was present at Captain Dreyfus's degradation. This event upset him greatly and the following year he published *The Jewish State: An Essay on a Modern Solution to the Jewish Problem,* in which he expressed his desire to "normalize" Jews through politics. In 1897 he called the first congress in Basel as a result of which the Zionist Organization was formed. Herzl was counting on diplomacy to grant him "a small piece of the Earth's surface" where he might establish a Jewish homeland, the hub of the future independent state. His approaches to the Ottoman Sultan and the German Kaiser failed. Having first considered Argentina, then Cyprus, in 1903 London offered Uganda to the Zionist Organization to establish their homeland. This was a great victory for the Zionists because it gave them their first international recognition. In 1903 the plan was ratified by the Congress with a small majority, but was immediately thrown out upon Herzl's death: Zionism only made sense in Zion! The Zionist movement was itself divided over its ultimate objectives. Ahad Ha'am (1856–1927), believed in a "cultural" Zionism, and that Israel had to become a refuge for Judaism. For him, it was not so much a question of "preparing the land for the people, as preparing the people for the land." In 1909 he helped to found the

Hebrew University in Jerusalem. In 1902 with the advent of the Mizrahi Party, religious Zionism appeared: the Hebrews were only a people because they had been given the *Torah* and were expected to observe its rules.

Religious Zionists believed, in fact, that the two exiles had been caused by a failure to do so. They rallied the movement for tactical reasons, and hoped to re-orientate it in a religious direction. The initial failure of the diplomatic path that Theodor Herzl had initiated – and which was later pursued by Chaim Weizmann, the future first president of the State of Israel – ensured that at the heart of the movement there was a preponderance of "practical Zionists" who chose to infiltrate Palestine, illegally if necessary. These pioneers of the second "*aliya*" – among whom was David Ben Gurion – laid the foundations of the future State of Israel, which "revisionists" Zeev Jabotinsky and Menachem Begin dreamed of conquering by force, and enlarging to include the whole of Palestine and Transjordan. It is worth mentioning, finally, two minority factions within Zionism: beside the "territorialists" who remained keen on the plan to establish a homeland on virgin territory other than Palestine, there was also a left who called for class solidarity between Jewish and Arab workers, and for the creation of a two-nation state. ∎

Ph.© Collection Viollet

As a reaction to the Balfour Declaration, the Palestinian population stood up to the British occupation. A demonstration organized in Jaffa in 1933 degenerated and twenty-seven people were killed and 200 injured. That year Hitler came to power in Germany, and Jewish immigration grew in direct proportion to Jewish persecution...
Coll. René Dazy/Ph. © Edimedia

Two Nations in One Country

The Arab-Zionist, then Israeli-Arab or Israeli-Palestinian conflict came about from this misunderstanding – or rather this blindness – because in 1880 Palestine was already inhabited. The inhabitants were the inheritors of a culture that had evolved on that land for at least twelve centuries. Driven out by European anti-Semitism, the Zionist emigrants were determined to resolve their own national problem, but despite themselves they were to contribute to creating a new problem: that of the Palestinian people.

Since biblical times the history of Palestine has diverged from the history of the Jewish people. First Roman, then Byzantine, the country was conquered in 634 by the Muslim armies. As they were at the center of the Umayyad Empire, the Aramean people became quickly and profoundly Arab, and the Frankish kingdoms that were established by the Crusades of the twelfth and thirteenth centuries could not change this fact. As for the Jewish presence, it was always there, but the Jews were few in number and always a minority. The old *Yishuv* community, made up of orthodox Jews – and later anti-Zionists – was concentrated around the Holy towns of Jerusalem,

Hebron, Safed, and Tiberias. In 1882, Jews numbered only 24,000 in a total population of approximately 600,000 people, among whom were 70,000 Christian Arabs. The future mandate of Palestine was therefore divided between the South of the Sandjak of Beirut and the Sandjak of Jerusalem. At the end of the nineteenth century, nationalist ideology was still in limbo in this part of the Ottoman Empire and mainly manifested itself in opposition to European domination. The Western way of life of the Jewish pioneers contrasted greatly with the traditional background and there were inevitable upsets. The political implications of Zionist immigration were quickly understood: in 1891, prominent Jerusalem citizens sent a telegram to the Grand Vizier, which was a real cry for help. They asked him "to forbid the Jews from entering Palestine and buying land." At this stage the Jewish influx was far from large, and the Zionist movement had little structure; nevertheless the Palestinian population began to be aware of the two fundamental political problems posed by the immigration and the loss of their land.

LE PETIT JOURNAL ILLUSTRE

LES TROUBLES EN PALESTINE
Des Arabes fanatiques massacrent des Juifs dans les divers quartiers de Jérusalem.

Beginning with the second *aliya* (or "ascent into Israel") of the socialist pioneers opposition crystallized. In 1908, a new journal, *The Carmel*, appeared in Haifa; its aim was to denounce Zionism. During the following year there were violent disturbances and the first Jewish self-defense force *Hashomer* (The Sentinel) was established in Galilee. The energy of settlers who had bought land from absentee landlords, who frequently lived in Beirut or Damascus, worried the Palestinian peasants, all the more because the shibboleth of the "power of Jewish labor" seemed to be coming true. The separatist plan, which formed the basis of Zionism, found its corollary in Palestine: this time it was not a response to Western anti-Semitism, but to local power in Palestine. To the detriment of the indigenous population, a more dynamic society, born from the European Jews'

In 1929 the incident of the Wailing Wall (see sidebar) led to a flare-up of violence throughout the mandate: in Jerusalem, Hebron and Safed, 133 Jews were killed. The tragic irony was that most of the victims had come from the old yishuv; they were religious believers who were strangers to political Zionism, and who had co-existed up until then with the Christian and Muslim population.
Ph © /Edimedia

sense of dispossession, was being constructed on their land.

In 1882 Eliezer Ben Yehuda (1858–1922) created a new national language from the biblical heritage, and modern Hebrew became a source of common cultural identity for the Jewish immigrants who came from many different lands. Inevitably the adoption of this language only served to deepen the division between the new arrivals and the indigenous Palestinian population.

The Palestinian Mandate

On November 2, 1917 the Balfour Declaration made public the help which the British government had given the Zionist movement. Great Britain had many interests in this matter: besides the sympathy of many of its leaders toward the Zionist idea, and its desire to find a solution to the problem of Jewish refugees from pogroms in Central Europe, it also wanted to guarantee the presence of a stable bastion around the Suez Canal – whose economic and strategic importance had been reinforced during the war – and it wanted to confront France, which as the traditional protector of the Levantine Christians, also nourished ambitions in the Holy Land. Finally there was the need in this decisive year of the First World

The kibbutz of the pioneer socialists tried to realize the idea of collectivism and show the "supremacy of Jewish labor." By effectively dividing up Palestinian space, they laid the foundation of the future State of Israel. An aerial view of a farming community between Haifa and Jaffa in 1933.

Ph. © L'Illustration/Sygma

War to sway the somewhat pro-German Jewish opinion in Britain, for the Jews hated Russia because it reminded them of the pogroms.

This declaration, which promised the establishment of a "homeland for the Jewish people" in Palestine, made the collusion between imperialism and Zionism very apparent to the Arabs. For it formally contradicted the promise of an Arab Kingdom the British High Commissioner, McMahon, had made to the Sharif of Mecca in 1915, on the basis of which Arab nationalists had revolted against their Ottoman rulers.

After the break up of the region, which had been orchestrated in secret during the war by France and Great Britain – the famous Sykes-Picot Agreement – the Balfour Declaration ratified in the Charter of the Mandate on Palestine, seemed to the Arabs to deny their very existence.

The Palestinian Mandate, which was entrusted by the League of Nations to Great Britain in 1922, was the only one which did not provide in its statutes for the establishment of an autonomous government which represented the people. Given the British commitment to Zionism, London had no choice: such a government would have hastily put a stop to Jewish immigration – and thus, to the very existence of a

Palestinian nationalist feeling was forged out of the struggle against the British mandate, and especially from the struggle against Zionist immigration. In 1936 villagers showed their support for the Palestinian revolt with very clear slogans: "Palestine for the Arabs!" and "The homeland is our religion, we shall give our lives for independence!"

Ph. © Collections Viollet

homeland. Since the Palestinians did not have such a government, they were faced with the long term threat of a Jewish majority in their country. The guarantee of the "civil rights... of non-Jewish communities in Palestine" – that is to say the Palestinian Arab majority – which was included in the Balfour Declara-

THE INVENTION OF TRANSJORDAN

It was in 1921 that the British decided to create a Hashemite Emirate east of Jordan, in a vast desert region populated by Bedouins. Abdallah, the son of Sharif Hussein, had been harassing the French positions in Syria from Amman. Winston Churchill, the Secretary of State for the Colonies, offered him a throne by way of compensation and an annual stipend of £18,000 to uphold the peace. The British, who trained the Emirate's troops, kept a hold on the country, and thereby managed to consolidate their position in this area where Syria, Iraq and Saudi Arabia all met. This final territorial division was interesting. On the one hand it put an end to Ibn Saud's ambitions – he was forced to surrender Aqaba on the Red Sea – and on the other hand it limited the expansion of the national Jewish homeland. But in fact, the division was to increase the conflict in the area, and complicate matters further: by basing Jordanian claims on Arab Palestine, and the Zionist revisionists claims on Transjordan. Much later it would help to justify the famous "Jordanian option" supported by the US. ∎

tion, has ever since proved incompatible with the establishment and development of a national Jewish homeland. The contradictory nature of these undertakings was a sign of the problems to come. The anniversary of the Balfour Declaration has been commemorated ever since as a day of mourning in Arab countries.

Great Britain proposed to restrict Jewish immigration to the "economic absorption capacity" of the country. But this would not have changed a thing, since from a strictly economic point of view this influx of useful manpower significantly increased Palestine's overall gross product.

The problem was really political. Two radically different nationalisms had been brought together, and the ensuing conflict, whose basis had been laid at the turn of the century, could only grow worse as the national homeland, supported by the now powerful Zionist organization, became stronger.

*B*eginning in 1936, each community took up arms: here Jewish volunteers from the Yishuv *learn how to handle their weapons.*
Ph. © Collection Viollet

In 1922, after the initial difficulties which followed the establishment of the British Mandate, Churchill's memorandum recognized that "this [Jewish] community, which is both urban and rural, and has political, religious and social organizations, its own language and customs does in fact have national characteristics." He also insisted on the fact that "the Palestinian people would never admit that an external organization, of whatever nature, could assume the right to dispossess it of its country, and to threaten its political and economic existence."

In the same way that Jewish national feeling had been aroused by adversity, Palestinian national feeling was sparked by the struggle against Zionism. Islamic-Christian alliances were formed. In 1920

*S*ir Herbert Samuel, first governor of mandated Palestine, Emir Abdallah, and Winston Churchill at the Jerusalem Conference in 1921 (p 58).
Ph. © Edimedia

Palestinians called for an independent government, but somehow the circumstances were never quite right and opportunities were missed.

While the Jews built the framework of their future state stone by stone, eminent Palestinian families, whose traditional influence had grown since the end of Ottoman rule, became divided, and they rejected any attempt at compromise. By making the repeal of the Balfour Declaration a precondition for all negotiation,

In many respects the Arab revolt was like a proper war. In 1936 in the orange groves of the Jaffa region, British soldiers took part in mine clearance.
Ph. © Collections Viollet

the Palestinians condemned themselves to powerlessness. Through fear of putting themselves on an equal footing with the Jewish Agency, whose very existence they denied, they refused the proposed Arab Agency, and deprived themselves of any formal means of representation. The only person to make contact with the British was the Grand Mufti of Jerusalem who put a pan-Arabic and Islamic slant on the struggle (see sidebar) which was objectively harmful to Palestinian

The Haj Amin al-Husseini (1893 – 1974) was the greatest Arab authority under the British Mandate, although his influence was often considered to be unlucky for the cause he was trying to serve. Amin al-Husseini came from one of the most illustrious families in Jerusalem and studied at the theological faculty of al-Azhar in Egypt. Having left the Ottoman Army to serve in Faisal's troops during the war, he became president of the Arab Nationalist Club, which soon distinguished itself by the virulence of its anti-Zionist activities. It took part in the anti-Jewish attacks in 1920. Sentenced to ten years in prison by the British, he had to flee. But he was soon granted a pardon, and the following year he was designated the Grand Mufti of Jerusalem by the mandatory powers, and then, in 1922, he was made President of the Supreme Muslim Council. He thus became at one and the same time the leading Palestinian religious dignitary and the only official representative of the Arab people. The Grand Mufti's anti-Zionist stance was

heard far beyond Palestine. His position was more Arab-Islamic than purely Palestinian.

After the disturbances of 1929 which were provoked by the conflict over the Wailing Wall, he was thought to have inspired pogroms from behind the scenes. The 1936 revolt forced him to flee to Iraq. Supported by Berlin he played an important role in the 1941 coup against the British by Rashid al-Kaylani. After he took refuge in Berlin, Amin al-

Husseini served the interests of Nazi propaganda: he supported the recruitment of Muslim volunteers for Hitler's troops in the Balkans.

After being arrested in 1945, the Mufti had to flee yet again and managed to reach Egypt where he participated in the creation of the Arab League. To counter the annexionist

ambitions of the King of Transjordan in 1948 he announced "the Arab government of the whole of Palestine" of which he became the President, elected by an assembly which had been set up for this very purpose. But in 1952 the Arab League put an end to his government. In 1958 Amin al-Husseini demanded the inclusion of Palestine in the United Arab Republic which had resulted from the fusion of Egypt and Syria: Nasser refused this poisoned chalice, which would have obliged him to undertake the liberation of Palestine on his own.

In 1959, having lost all credit in the Arab world, he returned to Lebanon where he died fifteen years later. ∎

Ph. © Harlingue-Viollet

The Nazi "Final Solution" left six million Jews dead. The memory of the Shoah (catastrophe in Hebrew) haunted the conscience and made unthinkable any threat against Israel, the homeland of the survivors.
Ph. © Centre de doc. juive contemporaine

claims. Disturbances broke out and in 1929 they spread across the whole country. Thirty-three Jews and eighty-seven Arabs were killed. The Jews saw it as a "pogrom," the Arabs as a national revolution, and the British as socio-economic discontent.

There was total incomprehension on both sides. The new *Yishuv* saw itself as a "small island" afloat in an "ocean" of rampaging Arabs. For the Arabs the Zionist enclave seemed like an "abscess," a "bite" which was draining the life blood of the Middle East and preventing its recovery. A widespread anti-Semitism developed in the Arab world using Western stereotypes that had been previously ignored.

In the thirties, with the influx of refugees from Central Europe, among whom were numerous victims of Nazism, the *Yishuv* practically doubled in size; in

1935 it represented close to thirty percent of the Palestinian population. As other countries in the region gained their formal independence, the Palestinians felt abandoned, and foresaw a Jewish majority in their country. For them time was running out. In the

face of the British refusal to install a representative government, an Arab High Committee, created and presided over by the Mufti, called for a general strike and civil disobedience.

Towards the State of Israel

The Palestinian Arab revolt had begun. It would last for three years. Guerrilla forces, joined by volunteers from neighboring Arab states attacked the British Army and the Jews. The *Haganah*, the unified Jewish militia, fought back, and the *Irgun*, the armed branch of the more militant revisionist movement entered the fray. In 1937 Arab leaders called for a truce and a British Commission enquired into the problems of Palestine. Having clearly analyzed the situation, the Peel Commission concluded that the national aspira-tions of each of the communities were incompatible, and for the first time it was suggested that Palestine be divided into two states. "The First World War and its after-effects have revived Arab hopes of reliving their Golden Age, in a free and unified Arab world. In the same way the Jews are driven by the grandeurs of their own past. They are eager to show the world of just what the Jewish nation is capable once it is restored to the land of its forefathers. In these conditions national assimilation between Jews and Arabs is impos-sible."

Despite the opposition of a strong minority, the Zionist Executive accep-ted the partition plan.

The Jewish state of Palestine was proclaimed in Tel Aviv on May 14, 1948 some hours after the announcement of the end of the British Mandate. Fifty years after the Basel Conference Theodor Herzl's dream had become reality; but the following day Arab armies re-entered Palestine. A long war had begun.
Ph. © L'Illustration/Sygma

The Jewish and Arab states were divided into several sections, corresponding, more or less, to the distribution of the two communities. The Arab enclave around the port of Jaffa, south of Tel Aviv is worth noting. As for the Jerusalem-Bethlehem region it was set up as a "corpus separatum" and placed under international administration. But the partition plan was to become a dead letter and Jerusalem was divided in two.

From an historical perspective, the establishment, only thirty years after Balfour, of Jewish sovereignty over more than half the lands the Partition Plan proposed, was a tremendous achievement. For the Arabs, who had been the inhabitants of that land for centuries, it was a major defeat.

The revolt intensified. The British fiercely repressed any disturbances, which led to 4,000 deaths, mostly of Palestinians. In 1939 Parliament adopted a new White Paper which broke completely with previous policies: having agreed on the practical impossibility of partition, Great Britain decided to limit immigration to 75,000 over five years so that the immigrants would stabilize at about a third of the total population. Then a representative assembly would be formed that

THE 1947 PARTITION

- Territory (land) accorded to Palestinian Jews
- Territory (land) accorded to the Arabs
- International statute of Jerusalem

0   km   100

LEBANON

SYRIA

Acre
Lake Tiberious
Haïfa   Nazareth

Jenine
Nablus
MEDITERRANEAN   Jourdain

Tel Aviv   **PALESTINE**   Amman
Jaffa
SEA

Jérusalem   Dead Sea

Gaza   Hébron
Rafah   Beersheba

JORDAN

El Auja

NEGEV

SINAÏ

E G Y P T

Gulf of Aqaba   Aqaba

JERUSALEM: 1948-1967

Mount Scopus   Hassadah Hospital
ISRAËL

SHEIKH JARRAH   Hebrew University and National Library

GEULA   American Colony
■ Tomb of the Kings
ISRAEL   ■ Saint George Cathedral

■ Rockefeller Museum
Mount of Olives
Hassadah   Muslim Quarter
Headquarters
Christian Quarter   Dome of the Rock
Saint Sepulchre ■   Wailing
Wall
Hurva Sinagogue ■   ■ Absalom's Tomb
al Aqsa Mosque
King's David   Armenian   Jewish Quarter
Tomb ■   Quarter
Mount Sion   **JORDAN**
TALBIYEH

rman Colony
■
Gare

BAQAA

TALPIOTH   0   km   1

- Israel
- Jordan
- No man's land (1948-1967)
- Zone erected in 1948
- ■ Important buildings
- — Armistice lines
- ▬ The old town wall

would legislate on the future of immigration. It goes without saying that Zionist immigration would have been completely stopped by the Arab majority.

This time it was Jewish national rights that were endangered by the mandatory power. This sea change was the result of a cynical calculation: on the eve of the Second World War the British Empire could not afford to alienate the Arab countries who had been galvanized by the Palestinian revolt, and who might be susceptible to the anti-British propaganda put about by the Nazis.

The Palestinian Jews and the Jews of the Diaspora took action. They were scandalized that the White Paper had been drawn up at a time of widespread Nazi persecution. They organized illegal

After 1945 bridges were burned between the British Mandate and the Zionist Executive. Determined to obtain a state at any price, the Executive challenged the British, taking them to task on their contradictions: how could they claim to be in favor of a Jewish homeland when they wanted to limit further immigration? Ph. © R. Capa/Magnum

immigration and prepared to take up arms against their former British protector in order to win their independence. The size of the *Yishuv* would now allow them to do so. In 1942 at a conference in Baltimore, Maryland, David Ben Gurion clearly defined the conquest of the State of Palestine as the objective of the war: "We will fight alongside the British as if the White Paper did not exist, and we will fight

the White Paper as if the war did not exist."

The *Haganah,* the *Irgun* and the terrorist Stern gang *(lehi)* adopted a joint operational framework, and in October 1945 Ben Gurion, on behalf of the *Yishuv,* called for an armed struggle; this struggle was marked by some spectacular successes, such as the *Irgun's* destruction of the King David of Jerusalem Hotel, which was the British powerbase. Jews, Arabs and the British were astounded, ninety-one victims were pulled out of the rubble.

Great Britain sent reinforcements, but the discovery of the extent of the Nazis' genocide, and the presence in Europe of 100,000 survivors who were waiting to emigrate, rendered the situation untenable. Arms smuggling and illicit immigration channels were set up. In July 1947, the *Exodus* drama shook the world: this ship had arrived at the shore of Haifa with 4,500 survivors on board, all refugees from the death camps. It was turned back by the British authorities... to Germany. President Truman backed the Zionists, as did the Soviet Union, which was pleased to support this movement against British colonialism.

Great Britain had to make the problem international, so on November 29, 1947 the General Assembly of the United Nations voted for the partition of Palestine into a Jewish state and an Arab State. The city of Jerusalem was set up as a *corpus separatum*, and placed under international authority (the city was then populated equally by Jews and Arabs). The partition was complicated and not entirely satisfactory. The port of Jaffa which had been given to the Palestinian Arab State was completely cut off from its hinterland, which had been given to the Jewish state. The Jews, with just one-third of the population, were granted fifty-five percent of the territory, including places where a large Arab minority lived.

The day after partition the first Israeli-Palestinian conflict began. While the British gradually withdrew, the others sought to strengthen their positions in preparation for a seemingly inevitable confrontation. In this war, which as yet had no name, terrorist incidents increased on both sides. The massacre of the village of Deir Yassin, carried out by *Irgun* troops, was

Still glowing from his victory, the young leader of the Irgun, Menachem Begin, received a triumphant reception upon his arrival in New York in November 1948. The important Jewish American community which had been created by the refugees from the Eastern European pogroms, brought decisive support to the Zionist cause. Ph. © Keystone

a major factor in the subsequent flight of Palestinians out of the country.

Until March 1948 the struggle could have gone either way. But the supply of arms by the West – from Czechoslovakia in particular – gave the Jewish forces the advantage. The work of the pioneering Zionists who had built up a territorial and community structure over the last forty years, bore fruit. The defeat of the Arab states who entered the war after May 15, 1948, the official date of the end of the British mandate, and the proclamation of the State of Israel, proved it. Despite their numerical supremacy the Lebanese, Syrian, Iranian, Jordanian and Egyptian troops who were fighting in Palestine, were defeated by *Tsahal,* the new Israeli army.

The 1949 armistice frontiers gave the Jewish state three quarters of the mandated territory. Jerusalem was divided in two, and the international protection plan was forgotten.

Even before the end of the Mandate was announced Jews and Arabs were contesting the control of the territory. Both camps ignored the fine line with which the UN had divided the states. Below are Haganah fighters defending a bridge at the entrance to Tel Aviv.
Ph. © Edimedia

The Refugee Crisis

Jewish nationalism had defeated Arab and Palestinian nationalism: while the Gaza Strip was adminis-

THE MAIN WAVES OF IMMIGRATION

PERIOD	NUMBER	ORIGIN	CHARACTERISTICS
1882–1903 (1st aliya)	20–30,000	Russia	"Lovers of Zion"
1904–1923 (2nd/3rd aliya)	35–40,000 35,000	Russia Eastern Europe	Pioneer socialists
1932–1938 (5th aliya)	217,000	Germany, Poland	Intellectuals, Managers
1939–1948 (6th aliya)	153,000	Concentration camp refugees	Mainly secret immigration
1948–1951	687,000	Arab world, Central Europe	
1952–1960	54,000 165,000 75,000	Maghreb Egypt (1956) Central Europe	
1961–1964	228,000	Morocco	
1965–1971	81,000 116,000	US, Western Europe Latin America	
1972–1974	143,000	USSR	
1975–1989	230,000	US, Western Europe, Latin America, Iran (1979), Ethiopia (1985–1986)	
Since 1989	500,000	From the former USSR	1.5 million potential Soviet Jewish immigrants

*I*srael was built to accommodate waves of immigration (see table) which favored the constant growth of the Jewish population in Palestine (below). After 1948 the geographical origin of the immigrants diversified. In 1985 an agreement with Ethiopia allowed the immigration of the Falashas, "the lost tribes" of Solomon, who practiced an anti-Talmudic Judaism.

Ph. © Falla – Baitei/Gamma

THE EVOLUTION OF DEMOGRAPHIC RELATIONSHIPS IN PALESTINE

1882	24,000	Jews in a population of	600,000 people	**4**%.
1914	85,000		815,000 people	**10**%.
1922	84,000		836,000 people	**10**%.
1931	174,000		1,207,000 people	**14**%.
1935	443,000		1,843,000 people	**24**%.
1947	589,341		1,908,775 people	**30**%.
15 May 1948	650,341		2,000,000 people	**33**%.

tered by the Egyptians, Abdallah annexed the West Bank to his Emirate and this became the Kingdom of Jordan. The Palestinian Arab State stipulated by the partition plan did not see the light of day, as it was simultaneously a victim of the strength of the Zionist movement, and the inaction of Arab states.

The problem of the Palestinian refugees became increasingly apparent: 750,000 people among the 1.5 million Arabs of which Palestine consisted, left Israeli territory. "Driven from their country" according to the Arabs; "encouraged to leave by their leaders" according to the Israelis, their flight is still a source of debate. Whatever the cause, this massive departure was a godsend for the Israeli government, for it

The first session of the Israeli government at Tel Aviv in 1948, under the watchful eye of Theodor Herzl's portrait. It was presided over by David Ben Gurion who insisted that the Jewish state must be faithful to the history of the Jewish people and be respectful of Western democracy.
Ph.© Keystone

ensured that the new state would be Jewish. From 1950 onwards Israel had more than a million Jewish citizens and only 60,000 Palestinian Arabs. Despite the December 1948 UN Resolution, Prime Minister Ben Gurion opposed the return of the Palestinian refugees while at the same time organizing massive Jewish immigration, which was encouraged by

SOME DEFINITIONS

Hebrew: This term refers to the people of Abraham and to the language of the Old Testament: the fact that the Zionist movement chose Hebrew as the national language emphasized their historical affiliation and the legitimacy of their claims on the Biblical Lands.

Israeli: Every citizen of Israel is an Israeli; in fact Arabs, Muslims and Christians are Israelis. But not all rights are determined by citizenship, some are granted on the basis of "nationality" (religion).

Israelite: Taken from Mosaic law, this term was coined from a desire for assimilation and to escape the heavily charged connotation of the word "Jew," and to emphasize the uniquely religious, rather than nationalistic characteristics of Judaism.

Jew: Who is Jewish? This delicate question has been debated for such a long time both by those who consider themselves Jewish, and by the *goyim* (non-Jews).

Responses differ according to the criteria under consideration (religious, genealogical, cultural, etc.). In Israel, in particular, the problem has not always been resolved (see Chapter Four). To be subjective, the best definition has probably been that: a Jew is a anyone, who for one reason or another, considers himself or herself to be one.

Zionist: A supporter of the return of the Jews to Palestine; all Zionists are not Jewish, and all Jews are certainly not Zionists. ■

Israel's Law of Return guaranteeing all Jews from anywhere in the world the right to live in Israel and acquire immediate Israeli citizenship.

The Palestinians were very much the losers in the new regional order which had resulted from the war. The drama of the refugees who were waiting uncertainly in encampments for the victory of the Arab armies, was to polarize the conflict and to contribute to its continuation. In the eyes of the world the Middle East had become a real powder keg. The State of Israel had come about through violence. The Jews had won their right to a state by force of arms, but torn between a West from which they had flown, and an East that rejected them, how were they supposed to lead the "normal" life of which they dreamed?

The Jewish exodus was completed and the Palestinian exile began. Some 750,000 refugees from the 1947 – 1948 conflicts were to settle in encampments. On an arid plain between Jericho and the Dead Sea this refugee camp found itself under the tutelage of Abdallah's Jordan. Abdallah had annexed this part of the Palestinian Mandate, and it was henceforth called the West Bank.
Ph.© Roger-Viollet

Chapter 4

NASSER'S
MIDDLE EAST

FOR THE LOSERS OF THE FIRST ISRAELI-ARAB CONFLICT THE PATH TO VICTORY LAY IN UNITY. ONCE HE NATIONALIZED THE SUEZ CANAL, NASSER BECAME THE ARAB WORLD'S MOST POTENT SYMBOL AND UNIFYING LEADER.

The defeat of Palestine was momentous and symbolic: defeat by Israel became the driving force for unity, which became a fundamental element of contemporary Arab political culture. Arab nationalism was rebuilt on an ideology of struggle rather than of "renaissance." For the believers in this nationalism it was imperative to abolish divisions as quickly as possible, even more important now, at the time of independence, than it had been after the First World War. Disunity was the root cause of the defeat and only served to help both the great colonial powers and the Zionist movement. Only unity would enable the Arab nation to free itself from foreign domination and become a worthy inheritor of its historic past.

In 1945 the founding of the Arab League addressed the first objective of unifying the Arab position on the question of Palestine. But the Palestinian cause, although it was mentioned frequently, was no longer really the priority: "Arab unity is the way to Jerusalem."

These calls for unity mainly served to ward off a sense of helplessness and to mask the depth of the divisions. Geopolitical axes were established. The traditional opposition between the Saud family and the Hashemites, which had been revived by Saudi fears of Iraqi expansion toward the Gulf, favored the building of a Riyadh-Damascus axis, which Cairo would soon join against

On July 26, 1956 Nasser announced the nationalization of the Suez Canal. It was a major event in the history of Egypt and the entire Middle East: it became the symbol of new found national independence. Nasser's era really began with this master stroke, and joyful crowds celebrated this "birth of the Third World."
Ph © Keystone

The news of the meeting in February 1945 between the King of Saudi Arabia and the American President Franklin Delano Roosevelt provoked Winston Churchill's wrath. For years after the First World War the Middle East had been little more than a private hunting ground for the French and the British, but it now became the new theater for Soviet-American rivalry. The Suez Expedition was the last attempt by the two colonial powers to ward off their inevitable effacement.
Ph © Edimedia

Baghdad and Amman. These geopolitical constants withstood changes in direction and declarations of intent: Nasser was no less opposed to the "progressive" Iraqi regime of General Kassem than he had been to that of his predecessor, Nouri Said. And Syria and Iraq were never greater rivals than when the two "brother" Ba'ath parties were in power in Baghdad and Damascus.

The Consequences of the 1948 Defeat

In 1948 the fragile unity of the Arab League was shattered. The objectives of the so-called allies were very different. While the Mufti of Jerusalem wanted to "throw the Jews into the sea," the Syrian leadership dreamed of a new national order which would bring about a "Greater Syria." Ideally this would include both Lebanon and Palestine and even Transjordan. As for King Abdallah, who was supported by the British, he was happy to put up with the Jewish state on his doorstep provided that he also had his share of the mandate's spoils. Lebanon, whose recent independence was not very secure, wanted, above all, to stress its autonomy. But its lack of resources meant that it could only summon up 450 soldiers. Egypt itself was forced to thwart the Hashemite dream of the King of Jordan. Abdallah's defeat could be explained by his army's lack of preparation and the poor state of its equipment. Those close to Egypt's King Farouk were implicated in a corruption scandal which involved supplying the Jordanian soldiers with faulty weapons. This backstabbing helped discredit the Egyptian regime and eventually lead to its downfall. For one of the young officers taken prisoner in the conflict, disgusted by Cairo's negligence and the entire political system, was none other than

Gamal Adbel Nasser. At the end of the war he secretly gathered a small band of officers together and they prepared to seize power. They had to wait three years for their revolution, but it came.

The Palestinian defeat had shaken the existing Arab regimes. The more moderate had to strengthen their tottering legitimacy by making bellicose declarations: we will take revenge, right will triumph! The leaders were actually afraid of suffering the same fate as Abdallah. Abdallah was assassinated in 1951 òn the square of the al-Aqsa mosque in Jerusalem. He was accused of benefiting from the partition plan and suspected of wanting to sign a separate peace treaty with Israel. The Palestinians resented the fact that the King had forcibly incorporated them in his kingdom, thereby legitimizing the Israeli conquests.

In 1949 when the ink was not even dry on the Armistice agreements, Colonel Hosni Zaim's putsch swept away the Syrian parliamentary regime which had been tainted by defeat; having done this he then began a long series of coup d'états in the region: no less than thirty-five in twenty years.

Jerusalem's fate encapsulates the implacable nature of the Israeli-Arab conflict, and the divisions of the Palestinian mandate. Following heavy fighting in 1948 the Armistice line was drawn down the middle of the Holy City. Looking down from the Wailing Wall, the Jordanian guards were on constant alert, surveying the "no man's land" which separated them from the Israeli sector. Ph © Keystone

"**F**our years ago, right here, Farouk fled from Egypt. Today, in the name of the people I am taking charge of our company: this evening our Egyptian Canal will be run by Egyptians!"

When he announced the nationalization of the Suez Canal Company, Gamal Abdel Nasser made history. From then on the Egyptian *rais*, a supporter of non-alignment, became one of the most important people in the Third World, on a par with Nehru or Tito. The symbolism of the canal's nationalization was tremendous: for the first time a former colonized country had managed to regain its economic independence. Nasser became the champion of the Arab world. He decided to address nations directly, totally disregarding the leaders of "reactionary" regimes. Nothing seemed to stop him: he was instrumental in causing the Lebanese and Jordanian regimes to totter in 1958; he incited the Iraqi revolution and

imposed unity with Syria. But it would not always be so easy. The United Arab Republic collapsed in 1961; the Egyptian army became bogged down in Yemen (1962–69). As the Tunisian Bourguiba noted, "There had never been such in-fighting among the Arabs until Nasser decided that it was his sacred duty to unify them!" The internal situation in Egypt

was not much better: economic failures, the crushing weight of the "socialist" bureaucracy, repression on all fronts... The terrible defeat of June 1967 undermined the regime and sounded the death knell to its aspiration for unity. After leading the War of Attrition (1969–70) Nasser decided in favor of

the US Rogers Plan, and a peace process began. His international authority allowed him one final victory; just before his death he managed to bring about a truce between the PLO and King Hussein of Jordan. Despite all his failures, Nasser remained an absolute point of reference for all Arabs. At his funeral in September 1970 both his supporters and his opponents gathered together to mourn a man who had, for fifteen years, been the Arab world's most potent symbol. Nobody knew how to capitalize on Nasser's inheritance. Nasserism did not really exist – he had just been the right man in the right place at the right time, with a powerful dream of unity and the capacity to fight for independence.

After Nasser's death Sadat turned his back on the Arab world and led his country in another, more narrowly defined direction. And with the Camp David Accords, Sadat banished Egypt, the former backbone of Arab nationalism, from the Arab "nation." A new era had begun. ■

Nasser and the Free Officers

On July 23, 1952 because of the breakdown of the Egyptian regime and a state of semi-insurrection – the prime minister and the supreme leaders of the Muslim Brotherhood had been assassinated, fires had ravaged Cairo, there had been guerrilla attacks on British military bases along the Suez Canal – the Free Officers overthrew Farouk's monarchy and the political system, which was symbolized by the Wafd Party, which was discredited because of its inability to deal with the British.

It appeared that there was a "politically disastrous generation" in the whole region after the defeat of Palestine. These watchwords conveyed an equal condemnation of Zionism, imperialism, and "corrupt and conniving regimes."

The Free Officers were a disparate band: while some sympathized with the Muslim Brothers, others flirted with communism. Without dispensing with the existing ideology, Arab nationalism progressively became more defined, essentially based on the themes of renewed dignity and the right to progress. The benchmark was the program of non-alignment to which the US and the old colonial powers were to object. The struggle was soon set to continue. Great Britain provided the opportunity as it, along with the US, was trying to secure a regional alliance against the USSR by means of the Baghdad Pact. The southern belt was made up of Iran, Pakistan, and Iraq, and was meant to block the Soviet Empire's progress to a warm water port – and the Gulf. In the Middle East this fixation with the Soviet threat seemed absurd as they were still preoccupied with fighting against the existing colonial powers, and above all, against Israel. Nasser, who stood for resistance to all foreign domination, started a campaign against the Pact.

In 1955 a particular set of circumstances precipitated a crisis: Ben Gurion, who had been recalled to the Israeli government, launched a massive reprisal raid against the headquarters of the Egyptian troops in Gaza. Thirty-eight soldiers were killed, but most importantly the humiliated *rais* realized that his army was in no state to stand up to Israel. He decided to

The Free Officers were a disparate band. While some supported the Socialist model, others such as Anwar al-Sadat were close to the Muslim Brothers. Only a tentative nationalism kept them together (p 76).
Ph © Keystone

modernize his military hardware. At the Bandung conference in April 1955 Nasser, together with Tito and Nehru, created the Non-Alignment Movement and at the same time announced his support for the Algerian uprising and his hostility to the Baghdad Pact. What is more, the Western countries refused to give him the weaponry that he demanded. Negotiations began with the Russians through Czechoslovakia. This was a fateful irony as it was the same route that had been used to help the *Haganah* at the time of the Palestinian war. In September 1955 this most important agreement was made public: it brought over 320 million dollars, and among other things promised 120 fighter aircraft. Two months later a defense agreement was signed between Egypt and Syria which received similarly favorable treatment. This Soviet intervention shook the world order that had resulted from the First World War. The Cold War had found a foothold in the region.

The Suez Expedition

For Israel the new deal threatened to upset the balance of power. Ben Gurion immediately showed himself to be in favor of a preventive action against Nasser before the newly-delivered arms became operational: as a strategic prelude to the invasion of Sinai, Israel occupied the neutral zone of Awjah and forced out the UN observers. As for Nasser, he encouraged commando action to take revenge for the Gaza affront, and in violation of international agreements he closed the Aqaba Gulf to Israeli ships.

The entire region began to take up arms. Israel became champion of the Western camp and proposed military bases for the US. France engaged in a program of nuclear co-operation with Israel and became its main arms supplier. In authorizing the partially secret delivery of Mystère planes France hoped to open a second front against Nasser: for it wanted to bring down the man it considered, wrongly, to be the henchman of the Algerian rebellion. As for Great Britain, the prime mover of the Baghdad pact, it feared the influence of Nasser's propaganda on the

On the eve of the Suez expedition, Sir Anthony Eden, who had just succeeded Winston Churchill as Prime Minister, was fêted upon his arrival in Paris. Like his French counterpart, Guy Mollet, he was haunted by the memory of the Munich capitulation. This somewhat debatable historical analogy inflamed public opinion in Britain and France.
Ph © Keystone

Hashemite Kingdoms of Jordan and Iraq, on Aden and in the Emirates. Saudi Arabia, which was implacable in its hostility to the Hashemites, was therefore already a supporter of Nasser.

The elements of conflict were in place. Nasser himself provided the pretext. Egypt decided to build a high dam at Aswan in order to ensure its electrical supplies and its irrigation program. Nasser approached the US for help in financing this project. As Nasser saw himself as the herald of the anti-colonial struggle, he did not think in Cold War terms. Was not the US traditionally an anti-colonial power? On July 19, 1956 the White House's refusal was expressed in humiliating terms: "The State Department considers that the regime's instability, and the deplorable state of the economy prevent the country from undertaking such a project."

The reply was no less cutting. On July 26, 1956, the anniversary of King Farouk's downfall, Nasser announced the nationalization of the Universal Company of the Suez Maritime Canal: its revenues would finance the building of the Aswan Dam.

In Egypt this decision was met with enthusiasm.

In Autumn 1956 the 2nd regiment of French paratroopers dropped on Port Said. Angered by their defeat at Diên Biên Phû, overwhelmed in Algeria, Guy Mollet said that the French government wanted to crush "this apprentice dictator who addresses the countries of NATO in insulting terms, because France benefits from the understanding and support of these countries for the policy of peace and freedom that it is pursuing in Algeria."
Ph © Keystone

When Nasser came to power the prospect of the British troops leaving the Canal worried Israel, all the more because the Egyptians wanted to ban ships sailing under an Israeli flag from using the Canal. The Sinai campaign which began on October 29, 1956 allowed Israel to take a stake in the Suez Canal and to control the Strait of Tiran, the Gulf port of Aqaba.
Ph © Lipnitzki/Viollet

The canal, which was a focal point for anti-British resistance, also symbolized the potential wealth of the country. Had not Nasser invoked the thousands of Egyptian workers who had been killed on the project solely for the benefit of the occupying powers and the shareholders of the company? In reality the Company's concession was due to expire within twelve years, but the nationalization acquired a mythic status which far exceeded regional and national boundaries. Since Doctor Mossadegh's defeat in Iran (he was overthrown in 1953 after supporting oil nationalization) this was the first time that a former colonial country had recovered the attributes of its economic independence. As the historian Marco Ferro asserts, the nationalization of the Suez Canal represented "the birth of the Third World." A dynamic was unleashed which would lead ten years later to the creation of OPEC.

For the moment the event gained much prominence in Europe, but in a very different way: France and Great Britain launched a massive propaganda campaign comparing the nationalization to the "remilitarization of the Rhine." Great emphasis was placed on the strategic importance of the canal because two-thirds of Europe's oil came through it. They also claimed that international law had been violated, but this was untrue as it was the company and not the

canal that had been nationalized. Still, national honor was at stake.

The French were the most bellicose. The socialist government which had been defeated at Diên Bien Phû and was having problems in Algeria, decided "to stand up to this new Hitler" whose next objective was thought to be the destruction of Israel. As proof of this determination an aircraft carrying Ben Bella, one of the leaders of the Algerian revolution, was forced down. He was jailed in France, but later became Algeria's top negotiator. Most importantly Great Britain, Israel and France decided upon an international expedition. The aim was to gain control of the canal, and depose Nasser, whose regime was expected to crumble under the shock of the defeat. To keep up appearances Israel was cast in the role of the aggressor: *Tsahal* would attack and the Europeans would intervene to "separate the combatants."

The Suez expedition was also a war of economics: two-thirds of all oil destined for Europe passed through the Canal; it was an "essential Western artery." At the end of the conflict the clearing of the wrecks which blocked the canal, was carried out under the auspices of the UN.
Ph © Edimedia

On October 29, 1956 the Sinai campaign began. The Egyptians were immediately outflanked by the Israelis. Two days later the French and British governments delivered their ultimatum: the two sides must withdraw, not just to the international border but fifteen kilometers beyond the canal zone. The Israelis were in the Peninsula but nowhere close to the Canal, so the ultimatum affected only Egypt. This timing revealed the differing objectives: as well as Gaza, Israel wanted to lay claim to the coastal strip of Sinai up to the Straits of Tiran, which controlled access to the Gulf of Aqaba.

Beginning November 1st, the French and British bombed Egyptian airfields and, ignoring a UN resolution, dropped their paratroops on Port Said.

BEN GURION, THE LION OF JUDEA

David Ben Gurion ("the son of the lion," his own choice of pseudonym) came to symbolize Israel's struggle for existence. Born in Poland, Ben Gurion emigrated to Palestine in 1906 at the time of the second *aliya* of the pioneer socialists. In 1909 he founded *Hashomer* (the Sentinel), the first Jewish self defense force. With a combination of determination and oratory skill, Ben Gurion became leader of the *Mapai*, the Workers Party. He read the proclamation of the State of Israel on May 15, 1948 and became its first leader (1948–1953). A believer in the policies of *fait accompli* he opposed the return of the Palestinian refugees and any form of compromise. Convinced that Israel could only impose peace on the Arabs by force, he began the doctrine of preventive action, and led systematic reprisals against the *fedaiyeen*. A true father of the nation, his

presence was considered indispensable in periods of crisis. After retiring to his Negev kibbutz in 1955 he was recalled to lead a government where he assumed the two roles of Prime Minister and Defense Minister. Together with the French and British governments he planned the Suez expedition and launched the "Kadesh" operation. As the years went by, Ben Gurion's intransigent Zionism led him to favor his idea of *mamlachtiyut*, the almost mythical concept of the Jewish state, to the detriment of his previous socialist beliefs. On the eve of the Six Day War, for one last time, he joined a government of national union, making his participation conditional on the inclusion of his former sworn enemy Menachem Begin, the head of the "revisionist Zionists." Following the Yom Kippur War, he died at the age of 87. His country gave him a state funeral.

Ph © Keystone

Despite a convincing victory on the ground – the Egyptian army had been taken by surprise and hardly resisted – failure was to come on the international scene. The US disassociated itself from the expedition since it had taken place during President Eisenhower's re-election campaign which was centered around the theme of peace. Besides, competition for oil was at its height and the US did not want to sacrifice its pawn to the two former powers. Finally the USSR floated the nuclear threat. Isolated, first Great Britain, then France, backed down. Defeated by this world-wide opposition the two countries withdrew from the region and were relegated to the second rank of world powers. Eden soon lost power and Mollet's government collapsed and the Fourth

The collaboration between the USSR and the US in the Security Council enabled the UN to ensure peace. The withdrawal accords insisted on the presence of the UN's Blue Helmets (below, in 1959) in the Sinai desert. It was their withdrawal, on which Nasser insisted in 1967, that precipitated the Six Day War.
Ph. © Edimedia

Republic crumbled. The US and the Soviet Union took over.

Unlike its wealthy allies, Israel realized its objectives. Its army refused to withdraw from Sinai and Gaza unless they were replaced by the Blue Helmets of the UN, the front line with Egypt was neutralized, and access to the Gulf of Aqaba was assured.

Ten years after the Suez Crisis, on the eve of the Palestinian War, Nasser attacked King Hussein of Jordan who wanted to limit fedaiyeen activity in his country. Hussein replied that it was all very well to preach when Egypt was protected by a cordon of Blue Helmets. The escalation of tension which led to the terrible defeat of 1967 was also inter-Arab. Below a column of Egyptian prisoners in Sinai. Ph. © Capa/Magnum

However, although this semi-victory gave Israel ten years' respite, it carried with it the seeds of a new conflict. For Egypt had difficulty in accepting the different treatment meted out to the two sides; the Blue Helmets were not occupying Israel's territory, but they *were* occupying Egyptian territory. In the Eastern imagination and in that of the Third World, "the cowardly triple aggression" of France, Great Britain, and Israel anchored the Jewish state even more firmly in the imperialist camp.

The US did not know how to capitalize on the sympathy that its stance in the Suez Crisis had won among the Arabs. Nasser was not a communist, and would have accepted US support, but he was snubbed. But Eisenhower's so-called containment doctrine was similar to that of the "pactomania" which Nasser had stood against. The US, above all, wanted to undermine the prestige that the USSR had gained from its support for Nasser in the Middle East.

The Inter-Arab Cold War

The Suez Crisis had propelled Nasser to the zenith of the Arab firmament, for here was a man who had successfully stood up to the West. The era of the "rais" had truly begun. His populism, which found

expression on the Arab Voice, broadcast from Cairo, worried existing regimes.

The 1957 legislative elections showed a pro-Nasser majority in Jordan. King Hussein ignored this result and declared a state of siege; the situation was potentially insurrectional so in keeping with Western practice Great Britain came to the aid of the friendly regime. In Lebanon the following year it was American soldiers who intervened to keep order. On July 14, 1958 a popular revolution finally brought down the Hashemite regime in Iraq, and the "Marseillaise" was sung on the streets of Baghdad.

The Egyptian front stabilized for a while and the Israeli-Arab conflict was only in evidence on the Syrian border. The election had brought a pro-Nasser coalition government to power. Salah Bitar, one of the founders of the Ba'ath movement, became responsible for foreign affairs.

While all Syria's neighbors (Turkey, Iraq, Jordan, and Lebanon) aligned with Eisenhower's anti-Soviet doctrine, tension mounted with Israel. By December 1955 Israel had already launched a raid on Syria in order to dissuade it from pursuing military accords with Egypt. The CIA was suspected of plotting against the government with the complicity of Iraq. In this explosive climate, the Syrian government, capi-

talizing on the euphoria which had followed the Suez expedition, requested a union with Egypt. In February 1958 the United Arab Republic (UAR) was proclaimed. Was an Arab nation really under way? The Syrians began to support the Union less and less as they felt betrayed by the hegemony of Nasser's bureaucrats, and in 1961 the UAR collapsed. This first, and last, attempt at Arab unity survived only three years.

While Iraq's new team shared Nasser's ideas, his independence from the blocs, his Arab nationalism, and his quest for modernization, geopolitical forces soon gained the upper hand and Nasser and Kassem argued over the direction of the "progressive" front.

In 1962 the inter-Arab cold war was again apparent in Yemen, where a republican coup d'état had overthrown the Imam Badr. Badr's followers, who were supported by Saudi Arabia — which was now firmly in the American camp — were a threat to the new regime. The Egyptians flew to its aid, and in 1967 sent a large expeditionary force. They were soon bogged down in a guerrilla war.

Whatever the rivalries which undermined the progressive regimes, the USSR was prepared to support them. The Middle East became the preferred ground for East-West confrontation, with the Israelis and Arabs caught in the middle. The superpowers overarmed their respective allies and war became inevitable.

From 1962 on, the Egyptian expeditionary corps became embroiled in Yemen. Nasser was to know his own Vietnam fighting against these royalist mountain-dwellers.

The Build-up to the Six Day War

Egypt decided to resolve the aftermath of the Suez campaign for it considered that the internationalization of Aqaba and the UN control of Sinai encroached on its sovereignty. Once again the problem of Jordan's waters heightened tension, and this was accentuated by the arrival in power in Damascus of the left wing of the Ba'ath party who believed in outright revolutionary warfare and supported the *fedaiyeen*. The Israelis felt increasingly insecure, infiltrations had resumed, and there was much warlike rhetoric from the Arab leaders. Since 1956 the Israelis had adopted the doctrine of pre-

DE GAULLE AND ISRAEL

After the Evian Accords (1962) and the end of the Algerian War, General de Gaulle's policy of strict political independence from the Eastern and Western blocs forced him to maintain a policy of strict neutrality in the Middle East conflicts. On June 2, 1967, at the height of the crisis which precipitated the Six Day War, he condemned the aggressor. He denounced Israel, making reference to the David and Goliath myth. Israel was a "self-confident and dominant people." In his letter to David Ben Gurion in December 1967 he justified his stance as follows:

"I do not in any way deny that the closure of the Aqaba Gulf was unilaterally harmful to your country, and I am fully aware that you had a right to feel threatened, given the height-ened state of tension in the Palestine region, following the flood of invectives against Israel, together with the hapless fate of the Arab refugees from Jordan and Gaza. But I remain convinced that in going beyond the warnings given to your government, in due time, by the French government, in commencing hostilities, in taking possession of

Jerusalem by armed force, as well as many Jordanian, Egyptian and Syrian territories, in then practicing the repression and expulsions which are the inevitable consequence of an occupation that is really more of an annexation, in assuring the world that the conflict can only be resolved by addressing the current territorial situation

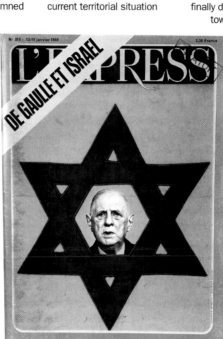

N° 914 - 13-19 janvier 1969   2,50 Francs

L'EXPRESS

DE GAULLE ET ISRAEL

« Ce sont les passions dont nous méconnaissons l'origine qui nous tyrannisent le plus. » (Simone Weil.)

rather than evacuating these countries, Israel went beyond the limits of necessary moderation. I regret it all the more since on the condition of your troops' withdrawal, it appears that a solution including the recognition of your State by its neighbors, guarantees of security on both

sides of the frontiers, which are to be decided by international arbitration, a just and equitable fate for all refugees and minorities, freedom of shipping for all in the Aqaba Gulf and the Suez Canal would today be possible within the framework of the United Nations, a solution which France is finally disposed to work toward, not just as a political project but also on the ground. This outcome would bring peace to the Middle East, facilitate world understanding, and, I think, would serve the interests of the people concerned, including yours. It would not, I know fulfill all your hopes... This is how Israel could become a state like any other instead of continually parading its moving two thousand year exile, and, as is common practice, its life and its duration would depend on its policies. And these policies will only work, as has been proven so many times, if they are adapted to reality." ■

(In David Ben Gurion, *From the Dream to the Reality.* Paris, 1986)
Ph © Edimedia

ventative attack; now, they applied it once again.

At the end of five years of extreme tension Nasser decided to close the Aqaba Gulf to Israeli ships, and asked UN forces to withdraw from Egypt – they could, after all, be redeployed on the other side of the border, in Israel.

It does not seem likely that Nasser, who was fully aware of Israeli military superiority, could have wanted the war. Rather, he foresaw a long drawn out struggle and liked to compare the State of Israel to Jerusalem, saying that like Jerusalem "this head of

At dawn on June 5, 1967 the Israeli airforce destroyed most of Egypt's potential military and strategic hardware. The war had hardly started and it was already over. Powerless Egyptian workers at a fire in an oil refinery near the Canal.
Ph. © B. Barbey/Magnum

the Western bridge will be destroyed in two hundred years time." He simply hoped that by keeping tensions high he would obtain concessions which would quiet things down.

Whatever Nasser may have thought, for Israel the closing of the Aqaba Gulf was a reason for war. On June 5, 1967 Israel claimed that there had been an Egyptian attack; this seemed quite plausible given the media build-up of the past few days, so the Israeli airforce went on the offensive. It was all over in a morning. Taken by surprise, the Egyptian fighters never left the ground. Having gained supremacy in the skies, *Tsahal* attacked on all fronts. In less than a week Syria lost the Golan Heights and Egypt lost Gaza and the Sinai peninsula, right up to the Suez Canal. Finally *Tsahal* took back all the Jordanian-annexed land the Palestinians had left after 1948, the West Bank and East Jerusalem. The Jewish state had tripled in size. The capture of the ancient city of Jerusalem was of considerable symbolic importance. In front of the Wailing Wall Moshe Dayan announced "This morning the Israel Defense Army has liberated Jerusalem... We are once again back in this holiest of

places, and we have come back never to leave again." His annexation of the city took place the day after the war, and regardless of international rights, it was seen as a consecration by the entire Zionist movement.

Israel was to keep its conquests. Unlike in 1956 the US clearly backed the Jewish state. They thought Nasser had gone too far in accepting support from the Soviet Union and thus bore responsibility for the conflict, and could best be balanced by embracing Israel as a strategic asset. They therefore applied their veto to a Soviet proposal which

The Six Day War began another exodus. Palestinians who had settled in the West Bank and Gaza in 1948 left for more welcoming lands; the Druze from the Golan Heights, which had been seized by Israel on June 9, 1967, took the road to Damascus as well, despite Syria's acceptance of the cease-fire.
Ph. © Magnum Photos

*O*vernight Israel tripled its size by capturing Sinai, the Golan Heights, the West Bank and the Gaza Strip. Although the Sinai peninsula was restored to Egypt in the Camp David accords, the colonization of the other territories increased in pace. The Golan Heights and East Jerusalem were officially annexed by Israel in votes of the Knesset.

demanded the unconditional evacuation of the Occupied Territories.

Strengthened by its victories, Israel hoped to open the door to peace based on its new territorial acquisitions remaining in place. But the Arab countries, who were gathered at the Khartoum conference, categorically dismissed its case.

A laborious compromise was finally worked out between the two great powers. Resolution 242 called for an Israeli withdrawal and establishment of "a just and lasting peace." It formed the basis of all future settlements. Israel was forced to agree to it, and Nasser and King Hussein also obliged. The Palestinians, referred to in 242 only in the context of the refugee problem, and the Syrians rejected it, thinking that it made a mockery of their national rights.

Despite this diplomatic advance there was a total impasse on the ground. After the ceasefire the two sides rearmed. In 1969 Nasser, who was coping with internal upheavals, armed the popular militia and started the "War of Attrition." This lasted a year, consisted of intensive bombardments of both sides of the canal and caused more deaths than the entire 1967 war. For nothing. The two sides remained entrenched in their positions, and various attempts at mediation came to nothing.

220,000 Palestinian refugees from the West Bank and Gaza joined the wave of

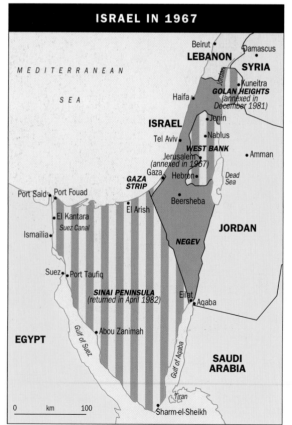

ISRAEL IN 1967

refugees from 1948. The Arab world was living through a new humiliation; all its certitudes were shaken, and it was faced with the myth of an all-powerful Israel. The balance sheet said it all: Egypt lost 10,000 soldiers and 340 planes, while the Israeli army, which had fought on all fronts, lost only 300 soldiers and about thirty aircraft. This was a small price to pay for the extent of its conquests.

One of the major outcomes of the Six Day War was a focus on the Occupied Territories. Because of this, the Palestinian question returned to the fore. While the Arabs, led by the Palestinians, gradually came round to the idea of co-existence with the Jewish state, Israel refused to co-operate. Now

Although Nasser resigned on June 9, 1967, and was then recalled by popular demand, Nasserism did not survive the defeat. The Egyptian people knew that Nasser's death in 1970 marked the end of an era, and they gave him an emotional farewell.
Ph © J. Burlot/Gamma

that Arab nationalism was in decline, the Middle East was in search of new ideologies, and Islam and oil were to become the preoccupations of the next thirty years.

Chapter 5

THE PALESTINIANS
CAUGHT BETWEEN
ISRAEL AND THE ARABS

IT WAS IN THE SIXTIES THAT THE PALESTINIANS FOUND THEIR POLITICAL VOICE IN THE PLO. THE QUEST FOR STATEHOOD IS A LONG ONE, AND PALESTINIANS HAVE EXPLORED MANY OPTIONS, FROM TERRORISM TO COMPROMISE, FROM THE INTIFADA TO THE OSLO ACCORD.

The 1949 armistice resulted in a divided Palestine in which half the Arab population became refugees. Overwhelmed by the defeat and the greed of neighboring countries, the State of Palestine, as stipulated in the Partition Plan, had not come about. Paradoxically the Palestinians were the main casualties of a war of which they had been the cause. For twenty long years, from the proclamation of the State of Israel to the Six Day War, their voice was not heard. This was because the other main Arab players in the war, chiefly Nasser's Egypt, had annexed their cause in the name of the superior interests of the Arab nation. Under Israeli and Jordanian occupation or under Egyptian administration, the Palestinian Arabs were reduced to silence. As for those who had fled the fighting or had refused to live under Israeli domination, they formed a miserable throng living in the refugee camps of the UN administration (UNRWA) that had been set up to help them. In 1950 UNRWA had 957,000 people within its jurisdiction; even by the Israelis' lower estimate of 600,000, it was still almost half the population of Palestine that had been uprooted in this fashion.

For its part the population of the young Israeli state had doubled in just three years from 1948–1951. This proved the continuing aspiration to the ideal of the promised land, particularly among the European refugees (the *Ashkenazim*); but Israel grew from the *Sephardim* as well, Jews from around the Arab world

In December 1987 the insurrection in the occupied territories was the expression of the radicalization of an entire generation who had been born under Israeli occupation. Taken up by the whole population the Intifada (uprising) made the position of the Israeli army untenable. As this movement proved impossible to crush by force Yitzhak Rabin – the "hawk" of the Labor party, – who had long been responsible for maintaining order in the occupied territories – was forced to recognize the existence of Palestine and to come to terms with the PLO.
Ph. © Chip Hires/Gamma

The Israeli people lived in a state of constant insecurity: between 1948 and 1975 250,000 people, almost ten percent of the population, chose to leave the country and set up home abroad. On the site of the old fortress of Massada armed men carry the ritual dais at the bar mitzvah of a young boy.
Ph. © Keystone

who had been encouraged to leave by the waves of anti-Semitism which followed the 1948 war and the Suez expedition: this was the case, for example, with the 100,000 new citizens who came from Iraq. This new exodus enabled Israel to reduce the problem of refugees to an exchange of populations, the Jewish immigrants compensating for the Arab refugees. The some 160,000 Palestinian Arabs who stayed in Israel became second class citizens with fifth column potential. They represented approximately fifteen percent of the population, and until the aftermath of the Suez expedition, they were subjected to a rigorous military regime. Half the Arab lands were confiscated and integrated into the Jewish homeland. This was done under various pretexts, exactly the same as those used after 1967 on the West Bank and Gaza. Then Israel segmented Palestinian space further by compelling only the Druze Arabs (who were ten percent of the Arab population) to undertake military service, which was required for access to certain social and economic programs.

Waiting for a hypothetical return, the Palestinians bore the weight of the defeat. The Arab states did not want to integrate the refugees any more than Israel. A

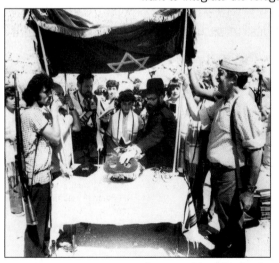

former director of UNRWA stated in 1951 that "The Arab states wanted to keep them like an open wound, as an affront to the United Nations and as a weapon against Israel. The Arab leaders could not care less whether the refugees lived or died." Forbidden to return by Israel and forbidden integration by the Arab states (with the partial exception of Jordan), this nation of refugees was to develop all the characteristics of a diaspora driven by the hope of national restitution. In the sixties Palestine began to find its voice. It became opportune for Nasser to give Palestine a semblance of political expression because of the way in which inter-Arab relationships were evolving. The time was ripe for rebellion, because the Israelis had diverted Jordanian waters and tension was growing.

The first Arab summit which was called in Cairo in 1964 to discuss a response to this action, charged Ahmad Shoukeiri, a politician with links to both Saudi Arabia and Egypt, with setting up the Palestinian Liberation Organization. This version of the PLO was a mere propaganda tool; its objectives did not even include setting up a Palestinian state, for it had been created under the auspices of the Arab League and Nasser, whose main aim at the moment was to outflank the Iraqis.

The Birth of the PLO

And so the Palestinians themselves had to take the initiative. At the end of the fifties, Yasir Arafat, Abu Jihad, Abu Iyad and a handful of militant refugees from Kuwait founded "Fatah," or the victory. By insisting that the liberation of Palestine was a precondition of Arab unity, the movement set itself apart, very much on the fringe of Shoukeiri's official PLO. Faced with the impo-

RESOLUTION 242 (NOVEMBER 22, 1967)

The Security Council, expressing its continuing concern with the grave situation in the Middle East...
1. Affirms that the fulfillment of Charter principles requires the establishment of a just and lasting peace in the Middle East which should include the application of both the following principles:
i) Withdrawal of Israeli armed forces from territories occupied in the recent conflict;
ii) Termination of all claims or states of belligerency and respect for, and acknowledgement of the sovereignty, territorial integrity and political independence of every State in the area and their right to live in peace within secure and recognized boundaries free of threats or acts of force;
2. Affirms further the necessity,
a) For guaranteeing freedom of navigation through international waterways in the area;
b) For achieving a just settlement for the refugee problem;
c) For guaranteeing the territorial inviolability and political independence of every state in the area, through measures including the establishment of demilitarized zones...
Although Israel and the Arab countries accepted resolution 242 (each interpreting it in very different ways) the PLO condemned it because it did not address the question of the Palestinian people's right to self-determination. They were reduced to a simple "refugee problem." ■

Resolution 338, which was passed at the end of the Yom Kippur War, reaffirmed the principles of resolution 242.

In 1969 the PLO adopted a maximalist strategy which was given voice in its constitutional Charter.
6. Jews who were normally resident in Palestine up to the beginning of the Zionist invasion are Palestinians.
9. Armed struggle is the only way of liberating Palestine...
21. The Palestinian Arab people... reject all alternatives to the total liberation of Palestine.
This Charter was declared null and void by Arafat in 1989, confirming the PLO's change of direction.
PH. © Keystone

tence of the Arab armies, Fatah wanted to resume the commando attacks which had not been used since the Suez expedition. Fatah believed that the only way to liberate occupied Arab Palestine was by armed struggle. On New Year's Day in 1965 Fatah launched its first operation on Israeli territory.

Its initial action, which contrasted greatly with the surrounding inertia, soon led to others; the commandos who had infiltrated Israel increased in number, heightening the tension which preceded the Six Day War. The defeat of the Arab armies was also a defeat for Nasserism, and it justified Fatah's method of approach. They now wanted to build an independent Palestinian state.

Although military resistance did not take root in the occupied territories – except in Gaza where it took the Israeli army three years to defeat it – the actions of neighboring states, and the recourse to international terrorism made the Palestinian question impossible to ignore. Shoukeiri was discredited and the armed resistance movements, with Yasir Arafat's Fatah at their head, took control of the PLO which claimed, from now on, its autonomy.

In 1968 the story of the battle of Karameh increased the popularity of the *fedaiyeen*: this small Jordanian village heroically resisted an Israeli reprisal raid. Karameh came to symbolize the new direction of the PLO. The organization, which from now on was heavily financed by the Arab states, especially the Gulf States, soon became the richest national liberation movement in the world. As the years went by it became somewhat bureaucratic. The Palestine National Council (PNC) which elected its executive committee, played the role of parliament in exile. Armed organizations, socio-professional groups and Palestinian communities from five continents were represented on it. The PLO, which prided itself on being the only democratic orga-

nization in the Arab world, became an enormous bureaucracy, with numerous departments from Health (the Palestine Red Crescent) to Foreign Affairs. They simply need-
ed a territory.

International Terrorism

The PLO gained international celebrity by extremely
dubious means: in 1968 an Israeli El Al airliner was
attacked at the Athens airport by a *fedaiyeen* commando. This new form of international terrorism was
born and was well served by the worldwide media.

In February 1970 a Swiss airplane bound for Tel Aviv
exploded in mid-air, killing forty-seven people. Two years
later, the massacre of the passengers of an Air France
flight at the Lod Airport by a commando from the
Japanese Red Army shocked the world. There was a further escalation of terrorism in September of the same
year, when the Black September Group assassinated
twelve Israeli athletes at the Munich Olympic Games.
Israel's response was no less deadly. The bombing of
the refugee camps in Lebanon and Syria killed more
than 200 people. Black September demanded the

*From the beginning of 1970
there was palpable tension
between the fedaiyeen and the
Jordanian government. The
hijacking of a plane at Zarka
airport in the north of the
Kingdom was the last straw: the
guerillas stamped the
passengers' passports with
Palestinian visas and openly
defied the king's authority.
Ph. © Keystone*

Over the years France became one of the theaters of Middle Eastern terrorism. While the settling of Palestinian scores was initially at the forefront, these were progressively supplanted by the Armenian struggle, the Iran-Iraq conflict, and the wars in Lebanon.

release of the same number of Palestinian prisoners in Israel.

The involvement of the Arab states added another element to this deadly cocktail: Egypt, Iraq and Algeria all provided logistical support to the Palestinian commandos. In the eighties Libya, Syria and Iran took over this role. Since it was considered to be an act of war, terrorism provoked an immediate response from the states it targeted. On October 1, 1985 the Israeli air-force bombed the headquarters of the PLO in Tunis, following the murder of three of its nationals. Just a half a year later eighteen American bombers dropped their bombs on Tripoli and Benghazi, punishing Colonel Qaddafi and, by extension, Libya, for their presumed complicity in an attack on a discotheque frequented by American soldiers in West Berlin.

The sword of terrorism was double-edged. In 1970 King Hussein of Jordan used it as a pretext to severely repress the *fedaiyeen* movements. The principal bases of the PLO were in Jordan, and the monarchy became the principal target of *fedaiyeen* recriminations against

TERRORIST ATTACKS 1972–1989

1972–3 Assassination of three Palestinian leaders in France: Mahmoud Hamchani (booby trapped telephone), Bassel al-Koubeissi (assassin) and Mohammed Boudia (car bomb). ■ **July 15, 1974** Attack in the Boulevard St. Germain in Paris: two dead (Carlos, a dissident of the PFLP). ■ **June 27, 1976** Hijacking of an Air France airplane at Entebbe (Black September Group). ■ **1977–78** Assassination of three Palestinian leaders in France: Mahmoud Ould Saleh (assassin), Ezzedine Kalak and Adnan Hammad (Abu Nidal). ■ **July 18, 1980** Assassination attempt on Shapour Bakhtiar, former Iranian prime minister under the Shah; Anis Naccache, commando chief, a presidential favorite in July 1990; Shapour Bakhtiar assassinated in Paris in August 1991. ■ **October 3, 1980** Attack on the synagogue in the Rue de Copernic in Paris: four dead, twelve injured (Abu Nidal?). ■ **September 4, 1981** Assassination of the French Ambassador in Lebanon, Louis Delamare. ■ **April 3, 1982** Assassination of the Israeli Diplomat Yacob Barsimentov (FARL, Lebanese Revolutionary Army). ■ **August 9, 1982** Attack on the Goldenberg Restaurant in the Rue des Rosiers in Paris: six dead, twenty-two injured (Abu Nidal). ■ **August 15, 1983** Attack on Orly: eight dead (SAALA; Secret Army for the Liberation of Armenia). ■ **October 23, 1983** Suicide truck attack on the American headquarters in Lebanon: 241 marines killed and the French headquarters: 58 paratroopers killed. ■ **1985** The kidnapping of Western nationals in Lebanon. ■ October 7, 1985 Hijacking of the Italian ship the *Achille Lauro*: one dead (PLF). ■ **Dec 27, 1985** Simultaneous attacks on El Al Airline counters in Vienna: three dead and Rome: sixteen dead (Abu Nidal "as a reprisal against the Israeli raid on Tunis on October 1.") ■ **1986** A wave of deadly explosions in public places in Paris, of which there was a total of five in the month of September alone: Thirteen dead and 141 injured (responsibility was claimed by the CSAPP, The Committee for the Support of Arab Political Prisoners). ■ **Sept 19, 1989** Mid-air explosion of a UTA plane: 171 dead.

those regimes who had surrendered and accepted UN Resolution 242 and were therefore, by extension, responsible for all the setbacks with Israel. The provocative slogan "All power to the resistance" reflected the PLO's efforts to build a sanctuary for the Palestinian revolution in Jordan and inevitably led to a clash with King Hussein. They were supported by a sector of the population – sixty percent were of Palestinian origin – and they took control of the northern towns as well as several parts of Amman. On September 17, 1970 King Hussein's army attacked the *fedaiyeen.* Despite their past assurances, Syria and Iraq did not come to the aid of the Palestinians. The fighting, which was extremely violent, ended with 4,000 dead and the expulsion of the PLO from Jordan. The Palestinian "State within a State" had miscarried. A few years later the same thing would happen in Lebanon.

The tragic episode of Black September led to the PLO's change of strategy in two seemingly contradictory directions. Terrorism increased, on the one hand – as much against the Arabs states as against Israel – but so

"The resistance movement is ready to make the Middle East an inferno; it is ready to attack all imperialist and colonialist interests, and all those who want to destroy our people's hope..." Expelled from Jordan after Black September, the fedaiyeen took refugee in neighboring countries, mainly Lebanon.
Ph. © Sipa

George Habash, leader of the PFLP, announces the freeing of the tourists who had been held by his organization in an Amman hotel in 1970. In February 1982 an announcement that he was going to France for medical treatment prompted a media outcry and a governmental crisis.
PH. © Wheeler/Gamma

did diplomatic activity. The object was to found a Jewish-Arab secular and democratic state in the whole of Palestine; this was the dream that Yasir Arafat revealed to the UN General Assembly in 1974. In order to realize this dream the PLO initially looked to Israel's Sephardim, who were in the majority but who had integrated unequally into the Ashkenazim establishment. The Israeli deputy, Uri Avneri, put forward the idea of a Canaanite federation which would regroup the Semitic people, Jews and Arabs, and would provide an alternative to Zionism – but it was not taken up. The Sephardim were to show their true colors by voting against the Ashkenazi-dominated Labor Party in 1977, bringing to power Menachem Begin's nationalist right-wing Likud bloc.

The Compromise Option

Always pragmatic, the PLO altered its direction as a consequence. In 1977 a majority came out in favor of a sovereign state "on any liberated part of the homeland." They were seeking an historic compromise based on the Palestinian right of self-determination, with, as a double corollary, the right of return, and the right to a truncated mini-state on the West Bank and Gaza with East Jerusalem as its capital.

The new political line, which was spurred on by the events arising from the Yom Kippur War, allowed the PLO to build on its diplomatic successes: it was recognized by the countries of the Arab League (including Jordan) as the sole representative of the Palestinian people, and it was heavily supported by the USSR. Most importantly, Yasir Arafat was invited by several countries to the UN General Assembly, where he waved "a gun in one hand and an olive branch in the other."

The "realistic" option did not come about without difficulties. The 1948 refugees, originally from Israeli territory, had difficulty accepting it and it was contested by the Rejection Front, which was led by the PFLP with the help of Iraq, Libya and South Yemen. Far from the actual battlefield, these countries wanted the guarantee of a certain revolutionary purity. If Yasir Arafat's option gained sway, rifts would deepen in the Palestinian Liberation Organization.

The PLO was actually a coalition of heterogeneous

organizations, a microcosm of the Arab world; the unified facade was only maintained by a maximalist charter which the organization later found it difficult to amend. It has been compared to an anonymous society in which each Arab country acted through PLO constituent organizations for its own ends: *Saika* was sponsored by Syria, the Arab Liberation Front by Iraq, and so on. For although the PLO was recognized by the Arab states, its fragmented nature worried them and so they made various attempts to contain it.

The Palestinian litany of complaints was long: Egypt's tight rein on Shoukeiri, Black September in Jordan; the Syrian army's interminable siege of the Tal al-Zaatar camp in Lebanon in 1976; the Siege of Tripoli, again in Lebanon, by the Syrian army in 1983; the massacres of Sabra and Shatila by Israeli-backed Maronite Phalangists; Iraqi and Libyan support for PLO dissidents or opponents Abul Abbas and Abu Nidal; the repression exercised against Palestinians after the liberation of Kuwait... As the poet Mahmoud Darwish put it, "We knew how far we had become Arabs in the Israeli prisons; we knew how far we had become Palestinians in the Arab prisons..."

The search for unity still seemed a vital necessity, however, for the organization only drew its legitimacy from its capacity to represent all Palestinians. Because of this Yasir Arafat's pragmatic leadership was often forced to endorse actions of which it disapproved. Hampered by its slow emergence as a coalition, the PLO became increasingly associated in the West with its extremist fringe; for many the PLO was not synonymous with nationalism but with terrorism, and this fact clouded the leadership's real efforts to engage in dialogue based on mutual recognition.

The PLO had never been in a position to control all the nebulous Palestinian fringe groups. As the years went by

A PLO calendar for 1983. In the Palestinian revolutionary imagination the dove of peace draped in the national emblem could only be associated with a gun, for this was the only way for these homeless people to make their voice heard.
Ph. © Edimedia

many of the moderate figures within the PLO were assassinated by those who waged war against "traitors to the cause." This was the case with Issam Sartawi, who in 1976 engaged in dialogue with Israeli leaders and was then executed by Abu Nidal's group – Abu Nidal had been condemned to death by the PLO in 1973.

In 1978 the ranks closed somewhat around Yasir Arafat's opposition to the Camp David proposals – they had been rejected by the Organization who had been kept on the sidelines of a process which did not recognize "the national rights of the Palestinian people." The PLO became reconciled with the Syrian, Iraqi and Jordanian capitals. Around the same time it tried to break with

In June 1982 Israel's invasion of Lebanon was directed against the PLO. After three months of bitter fighting in Beirut the Palestinian fighters had to withdraw under the protection of the French legionnaires. This was how they were driven from their last front line with Israel.

Ph. © Pierre Perrin/Gamma

the terrorist logic which could only harm its cause. It would now defend its cause by armed struggle against the *Tsahal* and by diplomatic action. The PLO wished to continue to win, rather than alienate, supporters.

But, traumatized by the bloody assassinations, the Israeli government adamantly refused to consider the PLO as anything other than a "gang of assassins." In June 1982 the invasion of Lebanon was purposefully directed against the Organization. The fifth Arab-Israeli War was, actually, the first Israeli-Palestinian War; in fact, it hardly provoked any reaction from the Arab capitals. A

THE JOURNEY OF A PALESTINIAN FIGHTER

In 1948 a young nineteen-year old Palestinian fought against the Israeli soldiers in Palestine. Forty years later in January 1989 at an extraordinary session of the UN, Yasir Arafat, President of the State of Palestine, solemnly recognized the State of Israel. An incredible distance had been covered between these two dates. A symbol of national resistance for some, a terrorist for others, Yasir Arafat's character is complex and difficult to understand, a product, perhaps, of a long and tortuous exile. His life becomes confused with that of the Palestinian struggle in all its dimensions. After 1948 he took refuge in Egypt and his militancy in Palestinian student organizations there earned him a brief spell in prison. It was the time of triumphant Arab nationalism and Arafat had a healthy mistrust of the Arab leaders who, like the Egyptian Nasser, hijacked the Palestinian cause for their own ends. This determined his future political strategy: if necessary the Palestinians should stand against the Arab countries and calls for pan-Arab unity, and should become self-determining. Constricted by Nasser's regime, Yasir Arafat moved to Kuwait. In 1959 he was one of the founders of Fatah. The Six Day War revealed the Arab countries' inability to lead the struggle and justified Fatah's choice of direction. Yasir Arafat made secret incursions into the occupied West Bank, and although he did not manage to provoke an armed uprising in the territories, the Organization did achieve growing support in the refugee camps. In 1969

Fatah took control of a newly rejuvenated PLO and Yasir Arafat became Chairman. To foil the threats of his many enemies, "Abu Ammar," or "the old man" lived surrounded by bodyguards, always on the move, rarely spending the night in the same place. His long political and physical survival (when so many of his companions have been killed) has made him something of a myth. At his historical address to the UN in 1974, Yasir Arafat, who was wearing the traditional *keffiyeh*, symbolized to the world the Palestinian struggle, the errors of terrorism and the dangers of an often ambiguous diplomacy. He succeeded amazingly in maintaining contact with both the Israeli pacifists and the Libyan maximalists, with South Yemen's Marxists and the Muslim brotherhood in Syria, and with Egypt under both Sadat and Mubarak. Haunted by the specter of Hajj Husseini, he was obsessed with reaching a settlement. During the summer of 1993 he used all his influence to persuade the PLO to accept the principle and conditions of a compromise peace. Yasir Arafat was the only Palestinian representative who could dare to break the taboo, and shake hands with the head of the Israeli government. At the first Palestinian general election in 1996 he was elected President ("Raïs") of the Palestinian National Authority. But the path to an independent Palestinian state was full of obstacles. ∎

Ph. © Keystone

Between September 16–18, 1982 in the middle of occupied Beirut, militant Phalangists massacred nearly a thousand people in the Palestinian camps of Sabra and Shatila under the indifferent eye of Israeli soldiers. The Israeli commission of enquiry concluded that Prime Minster Menachem Begin, Yitzhak Shamir, and especially General Sharon, the author of the Galilee peace project, were responsible.

Ph. © Mingam/Gamma

US led international task force had to intervene to save 10,000 *fedaiyeen* who left Lebanon under Franco-Italian protection, armed with heads held high. Despite an unrelenting two month siege and bombardment of Beirut, General Sharon could not finish them off. In one sense this was already a victory for the Palestinians and Lebanese.

But the invasion of Lebanon brought to a head the contradictions that had undermined the PLO for a long time: while the leadership saw the urgent need for a negotiated settlement, a new Rejection Front attacked Yasir Arafat's followers. The Front was extremely marginal within the Palestinian ranks, and was trained by Syria, who itself wanted to evict the Palestinians from Lebanese lands. In 1983 Yasir Arafat was under siege in Tripoli and once again had to leave Lebanon for Tunis, protected by France against the dual threat of the Syrian artillery and the Israeli navy.

Now the PLO no longer had a sanctuary. It was vulnerable, and found it impossible to retaliate after the 1985 Israeli raid on its headquarters in Tunis.

The Colonization of the Occupied Territories

This was how the conflict was referred to in the territories that Israel had conquered in 1967. When the fighting ended the Israeli minister Yigal Allon had advocated the colonization of a strip of land twenty kilometers wide along the Jordan Valley; this buffer zone was intended to prevent *fedaiyeen* raids but also to ensure Israel's deeper strategy. The *nahal*, an agro-military colony which had been conceived along kibbutz lines was one of the first forms of settlements. The numbers in the Israeli army doubled between 1967 and 1985 (from 71,000 to 140,000 soldiers) as much to ward off threats as to drive this territorial plan. When the Likud came to power in 1977 the colonization of the territories sped up considerably; they wanted to hasten the policy by "creating facts on the ground." The settlements were links in a precise geopolitical plan: the founding of *Israel Hashlema*, Greater Israel, of which Judea-Samaria (the West Bank) would be an integral part. The militants of *Gush Emunim*, the Bloc of the Faithful, were the backbone of this colonization. For them the recapture of land which had been usurped by the Arabs but which was Jewish by divine right, was a sacred task. Bizarrely, the neo-Zionism of these modern pioneers, apostles of a "return to God," echoed the theses developed by the Islamists in the opposing camp. Was this a sign of the impoverishment of secular Zionism?

The Palestinians used their demographic superiority

For many years the occupied territories were driven by the Intifada, with its cycle of demonstrations and reprisals. In January 1988 Israeli soldiers break up a protest gathering after the death of a Palestinian killed by the army in a Jerusalem suburb.
Ph. © Chip Hires/Gamma

(there were more than one and a half million of them in the West Bank and Gaza) to support their resistance. The settlements were originally conceived to house a million Jewish settlers. In 1994 more than 120,000 Jews were registered in the West Bank and on the Gaza Strip, 15,000 on the Golan Heights, and about 160,000 in Arab East Jerusalem. In the summer of 1993, just before the publication of the Israel-PLO agreement, the city of Jerusalem was careful to announce that in East Jerusalem the number of Jewish settlers (158,000) had for the first time exceeded that of Arab residents (155,000).

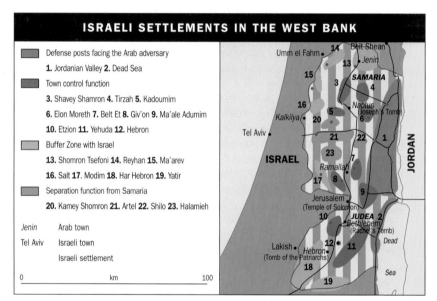

ISRAELI SETTLEMENTS IN THE WEST BANK

Defense posts facing the Arab adversary
1. Jordanian Valley **2.** Dead Sea

Town control function

3. Shavey Shamron **4.** Tirzah **5.** Kadoumim
6. Elon Moreth **7.** Belt Et **8.** Giv'on **9.** Ma'ale Adumim
10. Etzion **11.** Yehuda **12.** Hebron

Buffer Zone with Israel

13. Shomron Tsefoni **14.** Reyhan **15.** Ma'arev
16. Salt **17.** Modim **18.** Har Hebron **19.** Yatir

Separation function from Samaria

20. Kamey Shomron **21.** Artel **22.** Shilo **23.** Halamieh

Jenin   Arab town
Tel Aviv Israeli town
           Israeli settlement

0   km   100

The colonization of the West Bank began at the end of the 1967 war. If it was initially a response to military imperatives, it was soon adopted by groups of civilians who believed in a "Greater Israel." An economic logic sustained this colonization: attracted by the low costs, more than 160,000 Jews live in East Jerusalem and its suburbs.

The Revolution of Stones

In December 1987 the Intifada (Arabic for uprising) began. An entire generation had grown up under twenty years of Israeli occupation, and they were tired of military and diplomatic failures. This "revolution of stones" began spontaneously and took both Israel and the PLO by surprise. The lack of any perspective had led to further radicalism: a third generation had succeeded the eminent pro-Jordanians, and the new followers of the PLO were more and more out of control. Evidence of this was the growing Islamic Hamas movement which was created in 1987 with secret Israeli encouragment as a supposedly less dangerous alternative to the nationalist PLO, but which called for the destruction of Israel and participated in the Intifada without recognition from the PLO.

Repression, violence, counter-repression: despite the deaths of a thousand Palestinians within the first three years, nothing could crush this movement which merely gained strength from its martyrs. The situation worsened: "collaborators" were assassinated and Israeli civilians were attacked with knives. On the whole, however, the Intifada respected the orders of the PLO which did not want to become involved in another armed struggle that might very well put an end to the organization. The symbol of the stone expressed not only the young protesters' connection to their land, but also the poverty of the victims and the desire to keep the conflict at a certain level.

Strengthened by the Intifada, which was a marvelous propaganda tool, the PLO leadership finally took the plunge: in November 1988 the PNC convened in Algiers, and recognized all the UN resolutions on Palestine including 242 and 338. At the same time it acknowledged Israel's right to existence. It then went on to renounce all terrorism, and to announce the constitution of the Arab State of Palestine which was soon recognized by ninety countries. Another important development was that radical organizations such as the PFLP accepted the majority position. The PLO then began a dialogue with the American administration, the keystone of any settlement. But once again the intransigence of one side or the other halted the momentum. When a new Israeli government took office in Jerusalem, including some who were in favor of the forcible transfer of Arabs from "Judea-Samaria" (the West Bank), a small PLO faction attempted a military attack on a Tel Aviv beach. It failed, but the talks were broken off.

It was in this context of diplomatic stasis that the Gulf Crisis exploded. In the eyes of the Palestinians, Iraq had all the trump cards: a powerful army which aspired to strategic parity with Israel by matching chemical weapons against nuclear weapons. The country was one of the last bastions of Arab nationalism. The PLO gave in to the propaganda of Saddam Hussein who

Using the old settlement techniques of the Yishuv, colonization was undertaken in a methodical fashion. The objective was to divide Palestinian territory in such a way as to establish a new territorial continuity, this time for the benefit of Jewish settlers.

Washington, September 13, 1993. From both a media and a symbolic viewpoint this was a remarkable event: a photograph of the handshake between the two warlords, under the benevolent gaze of President Clinton, was flashed around the world. The Oslo Accord, however, posed as many problems as it solved. Soon the opponents of the peace process became restive. On November 4, 1995 Yitzhak Rabin was assassinated by an Israeli extremist.
Ph. © G. Merillon/Gamma

once again brandished the flag of the Palestinian cause.

Yasir Arafat's Organization was to pay dearly for its support of the master of Baghdad. The PLO was in a desperate position: it was excluded from the post-Gulf War Madrid Conference on the Middle East, which opened in October 1991, and it was ostracized by the oil magnates of the Gulf who withdrew all financial support. It was, however, its very weakness that enabled Yasir Arafat to re-establish his position. In Israel the Labor Party led by Yitzhak Rabin and Shimon Pérès regained power. They were eager to overcome the impasse on occupation since it was only nourishing extremism on both sides. In the territories the Islamic movements of Hamas and Jihad were gaining ground at the expense of Yasir Arafat's Fatah. Among the settlers Rabbi Kahane's now outlawed Kach and other racist imitators were gaining support.

The worsening of the Intifada hastened the process which had begun in Madrid. In the summer of 1993 secret negotiations, which had begun under the aegis of Johan Joergen Holst, the Norwegian Foreign Affairs Minister, ended: with an exchange of letters between Yitzhak Rabin and Yasir Arafat that formalized the mutual recognition of Israel and the PLO prior to the signing of a "Declaration of Principles" (see sidebar).

Meanwhile the Oslo Accord posed as many problems as it solved. Besides the confirmation of their mutual goodwill, the two sides could not agree on anything, and liaison committees became embroiled in byzantine discussions. The intentions of the two signatories were very different; while Yitzhak Rabin remained opposed to the creation of a Palestinian State, Yasir Arafat maintained this objective. The most important questions could not be agreed upon, and were delayed for future talks: the status of Jerusalem, refugees, the Jewish settlements, security arrangements, borders, and the nature of the Palestinian "entity." The setting up of a Palestinian police force also caused tremendous problems: as it was subject to Israeli authority it risked being seen as an adjunct to the *Tsahal* doing the "dirty work" in its stead.

Initial Palestinian hopes for a swift Israeli withdrawal could not be sustained, largely because of the Israeli

The Israeli-Palestinian Accord in September 1993 was made possible by an exchange of letters between Yasir Arafat, President of the PLO, and Yitzhak Rabin, Prime Minster of Israel.

9 September 1993

Dear Prime Minister.

The signing of the Declaration of Principles marks a new era in the history of the Middle East. With this strong conviction I would like to confirm the following undertakings:

...the PLO considers that the signing of the Declaration of Principles constitutes an historic event which begins a new era of peaceful coexistence, without violence or any act which might endanger peace and stability. As a consequence the PLO renounces all recourse to terrorism, and all other acts of violence and will guarantee the acceptance of all its members, warn against any violations (of this agreement) and sanction the offenders...

9 September 1993

Dear President,

In reply to your letter of 9 September 1993 I should like to confirm that in the light of the PLO's undertakings therein, the Israeli government has decided to recognize the PLO as the representative of the Palestinian people, and to undertake negotiations with the PLO within the framework of the Middle East peace process.

Signed on September 13, 1993 the "Declaration of Principles on the interim autonomy arrangement, stated in its preamble:

The government of the State of Israel and the PLO's leadership... representing the Palestinian people have agreed that it is time to put an end to decades of confrontation and conflict, to recognize their mutual legitimate and political rights, and to try hard to live in peaceful coexistence, mutual dignity and security, and to reach a global just and lasting peace settlement as well as an historical reconciliation by means of the agreed political process...

Above all the Declaration was an "agreement to agree" which began a mechanism which was to lead to the emergence of a global solution and the establishment of a permanent statute. The Accord came into force one month after it had been signed, October 13, 1993, with the following timetable:

• July 13, 1994: Final date for the re-deployment of the Israeli Army outside the populated zones, and the election of an Autonomous Council. Palestinians in Jerusalem participate in the election. The jurisdiction of the Council

extends to all of the West Bank and Gaza with the questions on Jerusalem and the Jewish settlements in abeyance. The council has a police force at its disposal, but Israel has responsibility for defense and the global security of Israelis. (In fact the first re-deployment took place in December 1995, though not in Hebron which was partially evacuated only in January 1997, and the Palestinian elections took place on January 20, 1996).

• Between December 13, 1995 and April 13, 1996: The beginning, at the very latest, of negotiations on the definitive status of the territories, as well as Jerusalem, the refugees, the settlements, the security arrangements, the frontiers and relations with other states. Despite a first session before the Israeli elections, negotiations were put on ice when Benjamin Netanyahu came to power.

• Between December 13, 1998 and April 13, 1999: a definitive statute on the West Bank and Gaza was to come into force. ■

"Let me tell you, Palestinians, we are destined to live together on the same soil of the same earth. We who have fought against you, the Palestinians, we tell you today, loud and clear: 'Enough blood and enough tears, enough!'"

Yitzhak Rabin
September 13, 1993
in Washington.

settlements. Those constantly expanding settlements, whose roads criss-cross the West Bank and Gaza and who rely directly on the Israeli military for protection, undermine the effective implementation of the agreement, starting with making the Oslo-mandated redeployments of Israeli troops more difficult. Since only a small part of West Bank land was turned over to the Palestinian Authority, opposition hardened and Hamas continued to hold the high ground. A UN agency estimated that it would cost seven billion dollars over ten years to rehabilitate the territories, not that much, admittedly, when set against the fifty-five billion dollars that Saudi Arabia spent in the war to liberate Kuwait, but international participation in the financial part of the accord was slow to materialize and the initial euphoria gave way to frustration.

The strength of the PLO had been to know how to preserve the unity of people, divided between those inside Israel, those living under occupation in the West Bank and Gaza, and those in the far-flung diaspora. The ambiguities of the accord exacerbated the differences between the leaders of the Organization who wanted to give up armed struggle, and those opposed to the agreement, such as the PFLP, the DFLP and especially the Islamic Hamas who challenged the direction of the Palestinian movement; between the representatives of the PLO in Tunis who had negotiated the accord, and the Palestinians from the territories who believed that they had paid in blood with the Intifada and wanted to make their voice heard. What is more, the Oslo accord ignored the question of the Palestinian Diaspora of 1948 and the hundreds of thousands of Palestinians in camps in Jordan, Syria, and Lebanon felt abandoned.

On the Israeli side there was also much opposition. Yitzhak Rabin's Labor Party was divided by its desire to forge ahead and the intransigence of the settlers and the religious nationalists. The Likud was itself overrun by an extremist fringe of settlers who believed that the ungodly government was not justified in ceding sacred Jewish land to Arabs, whom it likened to the Canaanites in the Bible. On November 4, 1995, Yitzhak Rabin's assassin would come from among their number. In fact,

extremists from both sides kept up the cycle of violence and weakened the peace process. After each attack Israel sealed the territories, which only served to worsen the lives of the Palestinians. Between 1993 and 1997, mainly because of such closings of the West Bank and the Gaza Strip – 339 days between 1993 and 1996 – each resident's income was cut by almost half. What is more, despite Oslo, the number of settlers in the West Bank and Gaza continued to grow: 88,000 in 1990, 106,000 in 1992, 151,000 in 1996, along with the rapidly increasing 160,000 or so settlers in East Jerusalem. On the other hand the portion of land administered by the Palestinian Authority remained the same: only six percent of the West Bank was under full Palestinian control, and twenty-four percent under joint PA-Israeli control, in January 1998.

When the Likud came to power in May 1996 and Israel once again adopted the politics of "creating facts on the ground" the increase in settlements in the West Bank and Jerusalem accentuated the Palestinian disarray. The dream of a Palestinian state, with Jerusalem for the capital, was fading. Many hurdles would have to be overcome before the Israeli and Palestinian people would learn to live together.

The policy of Jewish settlements on the West Bank had succeeded beyond all belief. The cost of the maintenance and protection of these Israeli zones stopped the implementation of the Oslo Accords of September 1993. In 1997 Israel's announcement of the building of a new colony, "Har Homa," the last in a string of settlements which were encircling the Arab part of Jerusalem and separating it from its West Bank hinterland, threatened the very basis of the peace process. Above, the new colony of Revana in April 1991.
Ph. © Shlomo Arad/Sipa

Chapter 6

FROM CAMP DAVID
TO THE GULF WAR

WHILE EGYPT WAS WORKING TOWARD A HISTORIC ACCORD
WITH ISRAEL, THE FIRST INDICATIONS OF THE IRANIAN REVOLU-
TION BECAME APPARENT. THIS WAS A SIGN OF THE TIMES:
ISLAMISM AND OIL WERE TO BE THE DRIVING FORCES OF FUTURE
CONFLICT.

"It is not true that the Arabs detest the Jews for personal, religious or racial reasons. They consider us, reasonably from their point of view, as Westerners, foreigners, invaders who have seized an Arab country to make a Jewish state... seeing that we are forced to realize our objectives expressly against the will of the Arab people we have to live in a state of permanent war." Moshe Dayan's statement following the Six Day War revealed his scepticism, largely shared by the Israeli public, about the likely success of a negotiated peace settlement. In fact all attempts at mediation undertaken since 1967 have failed, and Resolution 242, which anticipated the end of Israeli occupation of the Territories, was to become a dead letter.

This is what led the Arab countries to resume hostilities with a more limited objective: not to liberate all the territories occupied in 1967, but to make the conflict international, which would end the pointless stand-off with Israel and open the door to talks. The Egyptian army's task was to cross the canal and to hold its eastern bank, and the Syrian army was to climb the slopes of Mount Hermon.

The date of the offensive was fixed for October 6, 1973, right in the middle of the month long fast of Ramadan. It was also the day of Yom Kippur, the Jewish festival of repentance. When the initial surprise of the Arab armies' offensive had passed, two huge airlifts were set up, by the US for Israel and by the USSR

In January 1979, following mass demonstrations, the Shah of Iran's regime collapsed, giving way to the first Islamic republic in history. After the oil crisis this event stunned the world: the Middle East was one of the world's nerve centers where any crisis had immense repercussions.
Ph. © A. Mingam/Gamma.

On October 6, 1973 Egyptian troops attacked the West Bank of the Suez Canal and managed to establish the famous Bar-lev Line, which was supposedly impregnable. One of the objectives of this war had been achieved: the myth of Israeli invincibility was shattered. Below Israeli tanks en route to the Sinai front.

Ph © Micha Bar-Am/Magnum.

for the Arab countries. Israel soon took the initiative: General Sharon, exceeding his orders, deployed his troops on the west bank of the canal from where he threatened to surround the Third Egyptian Army.

This conflict led to a spectacular escalation between the US and the Soviet Union: the regional opponents did not respect the cease-fire, and the Soviets seemed to want to intervene directly in the theater of operations. The US responded by issuing a third degree nuclear warning on October 25. There were no real territorial gains – Israel only withdrew a few kilometers – and a cease-fire was finally imposed.

However this war was essentially pointless. Because of East-West rivalries the conference dragged its heels. The US tried to set the pace. Henry Kissinger, Richard Nixon's Secretary of State, achieved some success negotiating territorial withdrawals but the fundamental problem was ignored. In particular, the PLO, who had just been invited to the UN, was immediately sidelined.

Camp David: The Story of a Failure

It was this new threat of a stalemate that led Anwar al-Sadat to take the plunge. Nasser's successor wanted to achieve peace more than anything, so that Egypt could extricate itself from poverty and under-development. The massive hunger riots which had shaken Cairo in January 1977 had made him realize that the need to address internal inequities was paramount. Fully aware of American pre-eminence in the region, the *rais* made a spectacular re-alliance: in 1971 he expelled his Soviet military advisers. In playing the American card Sadat recognized the overwhelming power of the US in the Cold War, and hoped to reach a settlement under the auspices of the primary world power. In order to do this he had to break the strongest of taboos and engage in direct dialogue with Israel. This is how his historic journey to Jerusalem, which raised hopes around the world, came about in November 1977. After decades of conflict, would peace finally triumph? In reality, despite the Camp David Accords, President Sadat's initiative was to fail. Although he reminded the Knesset of the need for a global treatment of the conflict, the PLO and the rest of the Arab world refused to give up their demand for unconditional Israeli withdrawal. They were supported by the USSR, and this fact together with Menachem Begin's intransigence, dashed

NOVEMBER 20, 1977: SADAT AT THE KNESSET

" I decided to come and see you with an open mind, an open heart, determined that we can establish a permanent peace based on justice...
I tell you in all truthfulness that peace will only happen if it is based on justice, and not on the occupation of another's land. You cannot ask for yourselves what you refuse to give to others. I speak frankly, in the spirit which made me come to you today. You must abandon once and for all your dreams of conquest. You must also abandon the belief that force is the best way to deal with the Arabs. You must learn from the lesson of the confrontation between us. Expansion will not bring you any benefits... What exactly is peace for Israel? To live in this region with its Arab neighbors in safety and security. To that I say yes. To live inside these borders, sheltered from all aggression. To that I say yes. To obtain all sorts of guarantees which will safeguard these two points. To that request I say yes... Any discussion of a just and permanent peace will be meaningless, any measure that seeks to safeguard our lives in this part of the world in safety and security will be meaningless while you still occupy land by force of arms. Peace cannot be valid and cannot be built while you occupy another's land...
If you have found legal and moral justification in establishing a national homeland on a land which is not your own, then it is best that you understand the Palestinian people's determination to establish their own State once more in their country...
So I tell you, ladies and gentlemen, it would be illusory not to recognize the Palestinian people and their right to establish their own State, and their right of return...
As I have told you, there can be no happiness for anyone at the expense of another's misery."

Ph. © Sipa.

On April 25, 1982 the Israelis gave the Sinai back to Egypt. The plan of withdrawal which followed the Camp David Accords was completed in 1990 with the restitution of Taba, at the bottom of the Aqaba Gulf. This minute territory, only one square kilometer, had already been the subject of a dispute between the Ottoman Empire and the British in 1892.

Ph. © A. Mingam/Gamma.

Sadat's hopes. He agreed to a separate peace.

The Camp David Accords had two separate elements. The first, which was to institute Egyptian-Israeli peace in a true and proper manner, concerned the method of the Israeli retreat from the Sinai and its partial demilitarization – precisely what Nasser had denounced on the eve of the Six Day War. The second element foresaw negotiations which would give the West Bank and Gaza an autonomous statute for a transitory period of five years, at the end of which time it would be given a definitive status. It was this part of the accords which caused the most concern because the Palestinians in the territories had not even been consulted.

In the Occupied Territories hostile demonstrations punctuated the stages of the Israeli-Egyptian rapprochement. The Arab world, swept along by the "Steadfast Front" (Syria, Libya and the PLO), viewed Camp David as evidence of Egypt's abandonment of Arab nationalism and Arab unity, and soon ostracized Egypt and excluded it from the Arab League. Sadat's isolation played into the hands of the Israeli annexationists: for despite the accord's ambiguities there had been a real opportunity to make progress toward a lasting peace. In this sense Camp David was another missed opportunity.

But it also formed a precedent which would have lasting consequences. At the end of the 1980s the weakening of the USSR modified the rules of the

game: the rejectionist camp was forced to move on, and Egypt – though still bound by Camp David – was reintegrated into the Arab League. With the Kuwaiti crisis of 1990 all the protagonists finally came round to the idea of a "historic compromise."

The consequences of Camp David were as follows: The Palestinians had to face the fact that the most important Arab power had signed a separate peace, while the Palestinian question remained unresolved. Deprived of Egypt, the Arab world no longer had a focal point and the battle for leadership was wide open. Syria was too exposed to Israel, had commitments in Lebanon, and had internal problems: right up until 1982 the regime was in real danger of a total civil war led by the Muslim Brothers. Saudi Arabia? This privatized state under-populated and run by the Saud family like a pro-American holding company did not arouse much enthusiasm; the Wahhabite ideology to which it laid claim was very much a minority interest in Islamic countries. This left Iraq. In these circumstances Saddam Hussein was to try to mount a challenge. Served by a powerful army, his regime seemed like a buffer against the Iranian revolution which worried both the West and the Gulf monarchies. The latter were to dig deep in their coffers to help Hussein in his crusade against the Ayatollah Khomeini. This was again a reflection of the times: it was no longer Israel but

Islam and oil that were to be the driving forces of future Middle Eastern conflicts.

The Challenge of Islam

The severe repression which many morally dubious regimes had exercised, led to the emergence of radi-

On October 6, 1981 at the anniversary parade for the "October Victory," Anwar Sadat was shot and killed by an Islamic commando. Based on the economic crisis and tensions between the Muslim and Coptic communities the Egyptian peace initiative with Israel nourished many extremists.
Ph. © Al Akhbar/Gamma.

cal Islamic protests. These first happened in 1979, the first year of the fifteenth century of the *hijra:* with the Iranian revolution, with an attack on Mecca by an Islamic group hostile to the Saud family whom they called "those worshippers of oil dollars," and with the Mujahadeen in Afghanistan. The next year, an Islamic republic was proclaimed in Iran, which was soon invaded by Iraqi troops. Finally in 1981 Sadat was assassinated by a commando convinced that Sadat represented an incarnation of the evil Pharoah.

Contemporary Islam was opposed to imported models (secular liberalism, Arab or non-Arab socialism etc.) and their external (defeat by Israel) and internal (lack of democracy and persistent underdevelopment) failures. It denounced the West's (in which it included the atheist USSR) perverted ideologies and its excessive modernization. It wanted to be a clearly identifiable movement that could tackle the challenges of the age by returning society to

Islam. In many ways it could be seen as one of the final manifestations of the struggles of de-colonization: most of the Muslim Brother's followers came from the Sunni lower middle classes, the same people who made up the huge Ba'ath and Nasserite battalions in the fifties. The Islamists were able to occupy the ground left fallow by a state incapable of meeting the needs of the poorest. Some Islamists were financed by Saudi Arabia, but oil dollars did not account for everything. They opened schools and clinics and established support networks which increased their following. This sheer hard work helps to explain why political Islam is the only political movement truly able to mobilize the entire Muslim East: when at the end of the eighties the authoritarian regimes had been shaken by riots and forced into some kind of political openness, contemporary Islam won the ballot each time – the Muslim Brotherhood in Jordan and the Islamic Salvation Front in Algeria.

At the beginning of the nineties, in Egypt, as in Algeria, the authoritarian regimes which were the heirs of the Arab nationalist revolutions, found themselves confronted with Islamic disputes which were bound to end in violence. In Algeria in 1992 a putsch annulled the elections which would have brought victory to the Islamic Salvation Front. The ISF militants were repressed and the country collapsed into the chaos of civil war. In Egypt, President Mubarak returned to Nasser's methods and declared open war on the Islamists.

*F*aisal, son of Ibn Saud, the founder of the dynasty, ascended the throne of Saudi Arabia in 1964. But the primary oil exporting country in the world remained, more than ever, governed by an institutionalized and archaic tribalism.
In March 1975, Faisal was assassinated by his own nephew.
Ph. © R. Depardon/Magnum.

The Example of Iran

Iran's case is not typical because of the particular nature of Shi'ism and the exceptional figure of Ayatollah Khomeini. However, it is still today the most powerful example of a revolutionary Islamic regime, and helps to give a better understanding of the Islamic movement, both in its political mechanisms and its conflicting and ambiguous relationship with the modernizing West.

Led by Shi'ite clergy, the Iranian revolution was certainly atypical in a predominantly Sunni Arab world. But, for all the secular leaders of the Muslim world it was time to re-evaluate.
Ph © Setboun/Sipa.

Since the twenties the Persian throne had been occupied by the Reza Shah Pahlavi. In 1936, inspired by the Kemalist model of secularism, the Shah freed women from the veil. He believed that obscurantist Islam helped to keep his country in the shadow of the Middle Ages. Ascending to power in 1953 following the US-orchestrated overthrow of the nationalist Mohammed Mossadegh, his son was to follow the same great plan. But, the Shah's rapid modernization policy only served to accentuate economic and social inequities, and led to corruption and speculation. Situated at the gateway to the USSR, Iran under the Shah became a major player in the US's cold war system. It was Washington's policeman in the region: 30,000 American military advisers were based there. Iran's populist struggle against the imperial dictator-

ship was to be associated, with classic Manichean logic, with the struggle against the regime's powerful ally, the symbol of Western domination.

The dreadful efficiency of the Savak, the Shah's terrifying secret police, papered over the cracks in social stability for a long time. Although much of the secular opposition was dismantled at the beginning of the fifties, smaller leftist organizations continued to challenge the Shah's rule. But it was the Shi'ite clergy who seemed to be the only organization capable of mobilizing the entire country.

In 1978 mass demonstrations, urged on by Ayatollah Khomeini and galvanized by the blood of thousands of martyrs, brought down the discredited regime. Ayatollah Khomeini became inextricably linked with the Islamic revolution.

A refugee in France, the old man became the symbol of the 1979 revolution, which he led once he returned to Iran. He then put into practice a new theological-religious program, which he had elaborated in exile as a reaction to the "idolatrous" power of the Shah: the *velayate faqih*, or the "government of

SOME DEFINITIONS

Fundamentalist. One who takes his or her references from the fundamentals of religion. This can lead to attempts at reassessment and renewal, as was the case with the first Muslim reformers such as Jamal addin al-Afghani and Mohammed Abduh (see Chapter Two).

Integrist. Applies the literal letter of the law down to the last detail. The problem of adapting to modernity is not a principle theoretical task, and the point of reference remains the Golden Age of prophecy. At this time the Saudi regime perhaps qualifies as integrist.

Islamic. Refers to the Muslim religion (pre-Islamic poetry, Islamic art, etc.).

Islamist. This modern term came about at the beginning of the century when the traditional framework of

Islamic references came into conflict with Western values. Previously any such qualification would not have made any sense: you were simply a Muslim. For the Islamist, Qur'anic law is at the heart of all political preoccupations. These can be varied, and the law itself is open to many interpretations.

Jihad. Literally "Holy War for the benefit of God." The individual must first purify himself, and then those close to him, and then if, under threat, he must take a stand against the enemies of Islam. In the sixties, as a result of Nasser's persecutions, the Muslim brother, Sayyid Qotb, radicalized this idea and applied it to "unholy" governments. Terrorist groups who apply the term in this misleading way only

represent a tiny minority within the Islamic movement.

Muslim. Follower of the Islamic religion. To be considered a Muslim, it is enough to believe in the ritual phrase: "There is no other god than God and Mohammad is His Prophet."

Sunnism and Shi'ism. It is not merely a question of "revolutionary" Shi'ites and "conservative" Sunni: while Shi'ism developed numerous mystical and pietist tendencies, the Sunni desire for reform, notably embodied by the Muslim Brothers, helped to engender many extremists (Sadat's assassins, for example). Islamic radicalism is a social and political expression, not a religious manifestation in the strictest sense. ■

*"**D**ivine law and reason command us to no longer accept non-Islamic or anti-Islamic forms of government." Published secretly in 1971, Towards an Islamic Government expounded Ayatollah Khomeini's ideas. Below he is in prayer in his French residence of Neauphie-le-Château before his return to Iran.*
Ph © Keystone.

the scholar," which advocated that political life should be controlled by religious hierarchies, who alone are able (while waiting for the return of Shi'ism's doctrinal "Hidden Imam") to decide if the law conforms to the Prophet's revelations. It is worth noting that many of his peers did not believe in the theory of the "Vicariate of the Hidden Imam" and clung to a more traditional interpretation of the religion. Nevertheless, Khomeini's views were accepted in the new constitution which was ratified in 1979.

The constitution outlined a democracy with universal suffrage, and parties who were representatives of the people; however, the laws passed by parliament and the actions of the government were submitted to a religious council who decided whether they conformed with the Qur'an. Thus Ayataollah Khomeini, the "Leader of the Revolution," imposed his own direction on the regime. In 1988, though, Khomeini himself intervened against the Mullahs of the religious council whose narrow interpretation of the *Shari'a* was blocking all reformist projects. As a test

of power the Iranian experience not only posed a challenge to the West but for Islamism itself, and once again called into question Islam's ability to modernize.

In 1988, after eight years of a war that had left nearly a million dead, the Ayatollah resolved to "take the poison" of the cease-fire with Iraq. Only the Leader of the Revolution had the necessary charisma to impose this measure which had for so long been seen as "defeatist": for years Iran had demanded that first the "impious" government of Saddam Hussein must be brought down, and his responsibility for beginning the conflict should be recognized by the international community. In June 1989 there was a mass outpouring of grief at Khomeini's funeral. For despite the failures and the excesses of the revolution, the figure of Ayatollah Khomeini is still venerated in Iran, and despite many predictions to the contrary his regime has survived him. But his spiritual inheritor, the Ayatollah Khameini was not of the same religious caliber. Though it was tailor-made for him, the theory of *velayate faqih* became weaker and the "pragmatic" President Rafsanjani seemed to be the Imam's true successor. After Desert Storm he pulled off the masterstroke of normalizing relations with both Iraq and Saudi Arabia. In 1988 he began a policy of rapprochement with Western countries which has increased in pace since 1990.

In a true classical fashion, having known its own period of Terror – opponents of all persuasions, liberals, communists, Mujahadeen and Kurds were fiercely persecuted – Iran seemed to be at the start of a counter-revolution.

Attempts to export the revolution had failed. The weapon of religion, far from being a springboard to

THE KURDS: A FORGOTTEN PEOPLE

Although they comprise some twenty million people, this race of Indo-European origin, ranks with the Armenians as one of the most neglected after the First World War. In 1920 the Treaty of Lausanne delineated the frontiers of a future Kurdistan alongside Armenia. But, the plan came to nothing because of the Turkish uprising and Britain's desire to keep the Mosul oil fields within a firmly controlled Iraq. The Kurds found themselves scattered over three countries: Turkey (where they represented about nineteen percent of the population), Iraq (twenty percent) and Iran (ten percent).

Although a temporary Kurdish republic came about in Mahabad in the north of Iran, it was quickly dismantled by the Iranian army.

Because they were very divided themselves, the *Peshmergas* often found themselves manipulated by rival states. During the Iran-Iraq War, for example, Iranian Kurds fought alongside Iraq, while their Iraqi equivalents took Iran's side.

The fierce repression of the Kurds culminated in 1988 with the gassing of the village of Halabja by the Iraqi army. The international community, which was preoccupied with Saddam Hussein, took no notice. After the Gulf War,

and a new uprising against Saddam, the intensity and the ferocity of the repression provoked the intervention of the UN forces in the name of "the humane duty of interference." A narrow UN-authorized, US-protected zone was created in the north of the country to prevent a massive exodus of new refugees.

The status of this zone was uncertain. A *realpolitik* would suggest that given the hostile geopolitical context, it is unlikely that Kurdistan would actually happen. The division of Iraq had simply aggravated the imbalances, and revived the rival claims of Turkey and Iran. ∎

In many respects the Iran-Iraq War was reminiscent of the First World War. The Iraqi breakthrough was stopped, the front stabilized, and it became a trench war where neither side gained the upper hand. (Photo, p 125).
Ph. © J Pavlovsky/Sygma.
Wearing headbands which read "Only God is Great" (below) thousands of young Iranians prepared to martyr themselves in "human waves" which shook the Iraqi defenses.
Ph. © Manoocher/Sipa.

the Muslim world, had confined the Iranian model to the ghettos of the Shi'ite communities in Afghanistan, Lebanon, and Iraq.

It was also true that in the particular context of the war with Iraq, the concept of the *jihad* was continually used by Iran against its foreign adversaries. By its very nature it took the form of total defiance of Western democracies, trying to influence their internal political life by threats and blackmail.

Terrorism and the Fatwa

Denouncing the unilateral support of some countries for Baghdad, the Iranians began a terrorist and kidnapping campaign. Since France was the second biggest supplier (after the USSR) of arms to Iraq, Iran accused France of being Iraq's ally. This accusation was not without some foundation, as France was bound to Iraq by an enormous debt (it exceeded twenty billion francs at the end of the conflict) and therefore the French government was deeply committed to its debtor. Iran's "Islamic" terrorism was therefore knowingly used as a means of pressure: there was a campaign of attacks in Paris,

and French hostages were taken in Lebanon. Iran became skilled at playing Western democratic games: three French hostages were freed between the two French presidential ballots in 1988.

The Khomeini regime also began another "diplomatic" innovation: the *fatwa* (religious judgment) such as the one pronounced against Salman Rushdie in 1988. Rushdie had reworked elements of the Qur'anic tradition in his novel *Satanic Verses* – for example Iblis disguised as the Archangel Gabriel whispered polytheistic verses to the prophet. For this Rushdie was declared guilty of heresy and condemned to death by

THE IRAN-IRAQ WAR

Main offensives	
Main combat zones	
Oil pipelines	
Closed pipelines	
Oil terminals	
Kurdish population	

0   km   500

TURKEY

Ankara

Erzurum • Yerevan

Adana • Dortyol • Mardin

Lake Van • Van

Diyarbakir

Aleppo • Mosul • Irbil

Tabriz

Lake Ormia • Maragheh

Piranshar

1982-1987

Banyas • Tartus • Tripoli

SYRIA

1980-1982/1989

Soulaymaniah

Halabja

Kirkouk

Tehran

CYPRUS

LEBANON • Beirut

Sidon • Damascus

Haifa

Euphrates

Baghdad

1982-1987

Bachtaran

Qom

ISRAEL • Tel Aviv

IRAQ

Tigris

1980-1982/1988

Karbala

Dizful

IRAN

Isphahan

Port Said • Jerusalem • Amman

JORDAN

Najaf

1982-1987

Cairo • Suez

Eilat

Aqaba

Basra

Khorramchar

Abadan

1980-1982/1988

Chiraz

EGYPT

RED SEA

Kuwait

KUWAIT

Mina al Ahmadi

Kharg Island

PERSIAN GULF

Ras Tanura

BAHRAIN

Strait of Hormuz

SAUDI

QATAR

Umm Sa'id

Abu Dhabi

Aswan

Yenbo

Medina

Riyadh

UNITED ARAB EMIRATES

A R A B I A

the Imam. Quite apart from the particular case of Salman Rushdie, Khomeini created a dangerous precedent, for with this *fatwa* he ignored national boundaries and assumed the right to operate world-wide in the name of all Muslims.

This could be seen as an outright challenge to the West which faced tremendous difficulties in integrat-

THE RACE TO ARMS

1992	Total numbers	Defense expenditure	
Peace process countries		(billions of $)	(% of gnp)
Israel	176,000 (+430,000 reserves)	6.8 (+3 US aid)	11
Egypt	430,000 (+300,000 reserves)	2.7 (+2.1 US aid)	6
Syria	408,000 (+400,000 reserves)	1.2	8
Jordan	100,000 (+35,000 reserves)	0.54	11
Lebanon	41,000	0.146	5
Countries of the Persian Gulf			
Saudi Arabia	101,000 (+ 57,000 nat. guard)	16.5	12
Kuwait	13,700 (+ 20,000 reserves)	13.5	60 [1]
Iraq	380,000 (+ 650,000 reserves)	8.6 (1990)	21 (1990)
Iran	470,000 (+ 350,000 reserves)	1.2 [2]	2 [2]
United Arab Emirates	57,000	1.6	5
Oman	37,000	1.6	18
Yemen	60,000	0.9	9
Qatar	9,500	0.9	12
Bahrain	7,000	0.2	6

[1] Linked to rebuilding costs after the Gulf War   [2] Official figure, treat with caution

The enormous weight of arms expenditure, which was certainly underestimated by official sources, hindered the region's development and increased the risk of conflict. The Middle East had become the place for non-conventional arms, as was shown by the dismantling of the Iraqi arsenal after the Gulf War.

ing Muslim comunities in individual countries – Indo-Pakistanis in Great Britain, Turks in Germany, and Maghrebis in France.

This new Iranian approach was to alter the course of international relations. On the one hand there was the "duty of the *jihad*" which obliged Islamists to fight against those who were "corrupting the earth," and on the other hand there was the "duty of inter-ference" which was first asserted following the Kuwait War, to protect human and minority rights. These two "duties" completely overturned the princi-ple of non-interference in the internal affairs of a state, and were in opposition to the principle of the nation state.

The Disturbances Worsen

The Iran-Iraq War (1980–88) showed the ever increasing importance of oil in the region and the problems that it caused. The war was prolonged unnecessarily as the Western powers did not feel particularly threatened by this low key conflict, and in fact wanted to keep both countries weak. As a result, and despite the terrible toll in human life, they over-armed the two sides. The West only became worried when the oil fields were attacked and over 500 buildings were damaged or destroyed and they feared for their own supplies. In July 1988, a US warship in the Gulf shot down an Iranian airliner with 290 passengers on board; soon after Iran decided to accept the cease-fire.

The war was terribly deadly (over one million died altogether) and totally upset the balance of power in the region. Paradoxically, Saudi Arabia, which had only been marginally involved, came out of it the most weakened. Although the country had feared being caught up in the revolutionary fervor (it had a strong Shi'ite minority, most notably in the oil fields) this had proved to be largely unfounded. It had pushed its capacity for self-defense to the limit. Iraq set itself up as the protector of the conservative Arab regimes on the peninsula, and those countries brought Iraq their diplomatic and financial support.

Since its creation in 1981, the Gulf Co-operation Council (GCC) which regrouped the emirates around Saudi Arabia, took care to exclude Iran (which was in favor of an Islamic council) and Iraq (which wanted an Arab Council): this was a sign of Saudi Arabia's growing mistrust of its powerful Arab neighbor. It also mistrusted Yemen, with which there was a contested border. OPEC failed to disassociate itself from these local politics and was thus unable to set price guidelines. While countries with a high density population like Iran, Iraq or Algeria demanded strict production control as the only way to keep prices high, the Gulf monarchies who possessed exceptional deposits did not worry about exceeding their quotas. Their strategy was more to maintain and

The Lebanese Hezbollah were one of the few successful exports of the Iranian revolution. In 1985, 119 Shi'ite prisoners were released by Israel: it was one of the conditions demanded for the freeing of the French hostages.
Ph © Nachstrand/Gamma.

It was during the Yom Kippur War that the West discovered the strategic importance of oil, the world's primary source of energy. The Arab producers who controlled about a third of world production, quadrupled the price of crude – from three to twelve dollars a barrel – and declared an embargo on Israel's allies. By trying to control the rules of the game a handful of countries provoked a serious economic recession. In the 1973 oil crisis "black gold" became a weapon.

Discovered at the beginning of the century (the first extraction operations dated from 1909 in Iran), oil quickly became a necessity after the First World War, especially for the great powers. Because it was less entrenched in the region, France had to cede the Kurdish region of Mosul to Britain in exchange for a twenty-five percent stake in the Iraq Petroleum Company (IPC). IPC claimed an exploitation monopoly in the whole region which was delimited by a "red line." But the American companies, who were supported by their government, infiltrated the IPC, and negotiated a concurrent monopoly with Ibn Saud on the Saudi oil fields. After 1945 the Americans strengthened

their position. The "Seven Sisters" cartel (the largest companies, of which five were American) controlled ninety percent of the market, and realized immense profits. Royalties granted to the producing countries were, of course, minimal.

Little by little, however, the producers came to recuperate a share of this manna by insisting on the fifty-fifty principle; that is to say, each side had an equal share in the benefits. Savage competition between the various companies helped the oil producing

countries gain leverage. In order to overthrow the major players, smaller companies improved the quota-shares to the countries which granted concessions: in 1957 the Italian ENI offered to backdate to Iran seventy-five percent of its takings. In 1960 OPEC (Organization of Petroleum Exporting Countries) was created, at the instigation of Venezuela, Saudi Arabia, Iran, Iraq and Kuwait, to help the producing countries defend themselves and control price levels. In the face of a

boycott by the major companies, nationalization began.

With the 1973 oil crisis the sparsely populated Gulf monarchies found themselves with vast fortunes overnight: between 1964 and 1984 the oil revenues of Saudi Arabia increased fifty fold. As a result the center of regional power shifted toward the Gulf States. Stockpiling all this money, the Arab regimes became increasingly mercenary; some bought oil dollars, others bought weapons. Despite the slump in the eighties the importance of Middle Eastern oil is not likely to diminish as the millenium approaches. Most of the world's oil deposits have only a short life expectancy, and their production will soon be exhausted – in the year 2000 in the case of the US. The deposits in the Gulf total forty-five percent of known reserves today, and that share will continue to increase, for the "life expectancy" of the Gulf's oil is far greater than that of their competitors. By about the year 2000 they will be assured of more than half the world's production. Even more than in 1973, whoever controls the region will decide the fate of the world economy for the next few decades. Perhaps this explains the size and speed of the US response to the invasion of Kuwait. ∎

increase the flow of oil to Western economies, which then became dependent on cheap oil, as opposed to raising prices which might have encouraged energy diversification in the West. These two completely opposing policies reduced OPEC to impotence, and increased tension, particularly between Kuwait and Iraq. Before Iraq's 1990 invasion of Kuwait, much of their conflict was played out within OPEC.

Oil revenues only helped the non-oil local econ-

omies a little. The generosity of the Gulf states soon reached its limits; the share of Gulf wealth invested in the Arab countries did not exceed seventy percent of foreign investments, and became even lower in 1986 when oil's price per barrel collapsed and found its 1960s level again. Instead, the vast majority of oil dollars were invested in the Western financial markets, driven by the stock exchanges of New York or Tokyo.

Oil encouraged inflation and led to increased urbanization, a downturn in agricultural production, and the departure of millions of workers (Egyptians in particular) for the Gulf states. These migrations accentuated the demographic and structural imbalances in both the countries involved. Dubai, for

Created in 1960, OPEC (Organization of Petroleum Exporting Countries) could not rise above local politics: developing countries such as Iran, Iraq, and Algeria believed in keeping oil expensive and limited by means of rigorous quotas; others, led by Saudi Arabia, believed in a cheap, abundant product.
Ph © Salhani/Sipa.

example, one of the small oil-rich emirates, has a native citizen population of 80,000 and a foreign worker population of more than six times that (520,000).

Also in the space of twenty years, the gap between OPEC's poorest and richest nations widened dramatically. At the same time, debts had increased twenty fold (270 billion dollars). Following the oil counter shock in 1986 and the IMF's policy of adjustment, the national revenue per inhabitant dropped dangerously in the poor countries: $13,000 per year per inhabitant in Kuwait as against only $650 in Egypt. With the decline, many Arab analysts thought that the oil venture, began in 1973, seemed more of a curse than a blessing. It had succeeded in dividing the Arab world. The huge disparities in income, accentuated

A NOMAD BECOMES THE LEADER OF THE REVOLUTION

Born in 1942 to a Bedouin family from the Syrta region, Muammar Mohammed Qaddafi soon became a keen supporter of Nasser's Egypt. After graduating from the Royal Military Academy of Libya in 1965 he led a group of officers into battle against the royal regime of Idris Senoussi and the Western presence in Libya. Four years later, on September 1, 1969, he personally announced on Tripoli radio the fall of the old king. The "Leader of the Revolution" was twenty-eight years old. Libya immediately demanded the evacuation of the British bases,

expelled 12,000 Italians who were still living in the country, nationalized British Petroleum, and immersed the country in Arab culture. A fervent believer in Arab unification, Qaddafi was nevertheless not able to sustain any alliances: plans to merge with Egypt, Sudan, Algeria or Tunisia came to nothing. He was not helped by his weak demographic

position (only four million inhabitants) but, he was fortunate in his oil, and his own personal aura, although this was sometimes a negative. Qaddafi followed a policy of all out attack toward the Middle East, and Africa (Chad) which was often destabilizing. Accused of fomenting terrorist attacks, Libya was the object of an American bombing in 1986. Six years later Colonel Qaddafi was again at odds with the US for his refusal to extradite two of his agents who were suspected of causing the explosion of a Pan Am aircraft over Lockerbie, Scotland in 1988. ■

SOCIALIST PEOPLE'S LIBYAN ARAB JAMAHIRIYA الجماهيرية العربية الليبية الشعبية الاشتراكية

200 ٢٠٠

الذكرى الثالثة عشرة لثورة الفاتح العظيمة ١٩٨٢
13 th. ANNIVERSARY of the FIRST SEPTEMBER REVOLUTION 1982

Ph. © Edimedia

even further by the ostentation of the *nouveaux riches* of the Gulf, fostered frustration and anger at the injustice among the majority of impoverished Arab populations.

Iraq was also an oil rich country, but because of its war with Iran it became more indebted every day; it was seventy billion dollars in debt at the end of the conflict. Saddam Hussein thought that the oil monarchies for whom, among others, he had fought, should help him redress the balance. But they shied away from supporting a regime whose military power was so overwhelming.

On August 2, 1990, it was a deeply indebted, heavily militarized Iraq that attacked its small and very rich neighbor.

From 1969 on, Saddam Hussein was the strong man of the Iraqi Ba'ath regime. In 1980 he attacked Khomeini's Iran. Deep in debt and yet rich in arms at the end of the conflict, he then attacked Kuwait on August 2, 1990. In order to eliminate the Iranian front from the international coalition, the Iraqi president recognized the 1975 Algiers Accords on August 15, the very Accords that had begun eight years of war. One million dead for no reason. Ph © Pavlovsky/Sygma.

The Invasion of Kuwait

Quite apart from the oil context, Saddam Hussein, who had always been driven by dreams of power and geopolitical ambition, thought that Kuwait was his by "right": for this tiny, artificial emirate which blocked Iraq's access to the Gulf, had been separated by the British from the former Ottoman province of Basra (see Chapter One). In 1961 Iraq had tried to invade this city state and its integrity had only been preserved by an Arab dissuasion force.

With the help of Kuwait oil, Saddam would have been able to influence the fate of the global economy; so in his attempts to reunify the Arab world by force, he directly threatened Saudi Arabia. Despite its sophisticated weaponry Saudi Arabia did not have an army capable of taking on the Iraqi war machine, which, along with the Western countries, it had helped to create. As for the other Arab countries, with all their divisions they were incapable of forming a common front against Iraq, which had become, with the exception of Israel, the primary military power in the region. In fact, some Arab countries sided with Iraq in its substantive disagreement with Kuwait over oil pricing policies.

As the sole remaining super-power and the guarantor of the world's economic order, the US felt it necessary to intervene. On August 15, 1990, the US

*O*peration Desert Storm caused enormous Iraqi losses – more than 200,000 deaths – in addition to which the repression of the Kurd and Shi'ite rebellions were even more bloody than the War itself.

began to create a huge coalition and deploy an armada of 440,000 soldiers (300,000 of them from the US alone). This major crisis, the first since the collapse of the USSR, was just the time to test the new equilibrium, and to confirm the US position with regard to the USSR, Europe and Japan. Under the umbrella of the UN more than fifty countries joined the anti-Iraq coalition.

The pro-Iraqi stance of much of the Arab world can be explained by many factors, including: popular resentment against the oil states, the unfairness of North-South relationship, the long association of the American presence with imperialism and Zionism, fascination with Iraqi military power, and the Islamic arguments exploited by the self-proclaimed "savior" of the Arab world, Saddam Hussein, who soon achieved virtually prophetic status. All the diverse crises which had shaken the Arab world over the last forty years were to be found in miniature.

The US launched a massive air offensive on January 16, 1991, twenty-four hours after the expiration of a UN ultimatum. Next to the overwhelming military superiority of the coalition, Saddam's response seemed somewhat feeble: he launched Scud missiles on the Saudi oil fields and on Israel. By striking Tel Aviv Saddam hoped to provoke an Israeli response which would, in turn, provoke an Arab reprisal. But his calculations proved wrong: checked by the US, Israel kept on the sidelines of the conflict. With its economic potential destroyed, and threatened with bombings, Iraq was in chaos for a long time. Following the forty year cold war between East and West, this was the first conflict to unite the developed countries against a Third World power. It was a strange prelude to a North-South dialogue.

However, the Gulf War hastened the ongoing rebuilding of a region which had been badly affected by colonial partition. There were so many problems: poverty, oil, geopolitical rivalries, human rights abuses, attacks on minorities, the Israeli-Arab conflict, the Palestinian question, the crisis in Lebanon, over-arming, the threat of massive destruction – by nuclear weapons in the case of Israel, and chemical weapons in the case of its neighbors. Although the linkage that Saddam Hussein had tried to make between the disparate Western response to his occupation of Kuwait and Israel's occupation of the West Bank, Gaza and the Golan Heights had not met with complete agreement, it did make clear that only a settling of all such conflicts would lead to stability in the Middle East.

This responsibility fell to the US. In the Gulf crisis they had used their supreme power, and played all their trump cards, including the PLO, to try to solve the most urgent problem, and come to grips with the Arab-Israeli conflict.

If international law is to be respected in the Middle East and elsewhere, it is up to the international community and its most powerful members to ensure that the resolve they showed in support of the Kuwaitis is also demonstrated in support of other dispossessed and occupied peoples, including Kurds, Palestinians and Lebanese.

This first internationalized post-Cold War conflict mobilized all the resources of modern technology. American Patriot missiles against Iraqi Scuds. Civilians were the most frequent victims of these clashes. Ph. © Sipa.

Chapter 7

LEBANON AT THE
CENTER OF THE **T**URMOIL

LEBANON, WITH ITS ANCESTRAL RIVALRIES, BORDER PROBLEMS, SOCIAL AND INTERNATIONAL CONFLICTS, WAS A NATURAL BATTLE-FIELD FOR THE MIDDLE EASTERN CONFLICTS TO BE FOUGHT UPON. THE LEBANESE WERE CAUGHT IN THE FIRING LINE.

The Lebanese war initially seemed absurd and incomprehensible, but became increasingly tragic. In fact, there was not just one, but several Lebanese wars. This ancient land of cedars was caught in a cycle of violence which could only come to an end if the whole region stabilized.

The Mediterranean city of Beirut, a crossing point between East and West, at the height of its splendor. For a long time it was considered on oasis of peace in an otherwise hostile environment, but this image was destroyed by the 1975 war.
Ph. © Roger-Viollet

After the colonial partitions of the First World War Lebanon's "historical legitimacy" was always called into question, more than that of any other state in the region. In 1920, France, who had been given the Syrian mandate in the Sykes-Picot agreement, announced the creation of greater Lebanon (today's Lebanon). The delimitation aimed to ensure the economic viability of the small state of Mount Lebanon, and the protection of the Christian Maronites who lived there in the heart of the Ottoman Empire.

Syria objected and did not formally recognize the Lebanese State until May 1991. The local population objected as well as they did not want to become part of a state which had been designed to protect the small Christian majority.

The ancestors of many of today's Lebanese had gathered together in the mountains, which proved an ideal refuge for the heterodox minorities. In the sixteenth century, the Lebanese mountain dwellers had been made into an independent emirate and were ruled with a rod of iron by the Druze leader Fakhredine

Lebanon is a land of contrasts. The Druze have cultivated their warfaring traditions in Lebanon since Emir Fakhredine made it the first independent emirate in the sixteenth century.
Ph. © Roger-Viollet

(1590–1635) who developed economic and diplomatic relations with European princes such as the Médicis of Florence. Beirut became the capital. His power relied on the alliance between the small group of Druze, who had a well-established warfaring background, and the feudal peasant Maronites. For Lebanese historians this region was the first example of a Lebanese entity based on the symbiosis of minority groups. The tribal and sectarian ties worked well for the emirate. On two occasions (1840–1860, then 1975) when the state had become weakened, those minority communities rallied.

In the 19th Century, trade with Europe – most notably with the silk industry in Lyon – began an era of Lebanese economic and cultural prosperity. French was widely spoken. But, already the difference in demographic growth came out in favor of the Maronites. The Maronite-Druze balance was broken. This was a symbolic turning point: in 1834, Emir Chehab declared himself to be a Maronite, unlike his former ally Jumblatt. Influenced by the rivalry between Great Britain and France, the struggle between rival clans reopened sectarian rifts. For while Great Britain, an ally of Istanbul, supported the Druze, France, in the tradition of the Capitulations, supported the Maronites.

Small and Greater Lebanon

Beginning in 1840 massacres followed massacres. The division of the state into two provinces – one Christian and the other Druze, only accentuated tensions, which soon turned into genuine conflict.

A rebellion of Maronite peasants against the feudal lords (both Christian and Druze) began the great carnage of 1860, which the Lebanese still remember: in total more than 300 Christian villages were destroyed by the Druze and their Ottoman allies. France intervened. The powers agreed on a compromise to solve the problem of 200,000 Christian refugees in the small town of Beirut. This was the origin of "Small Lebanon," which was based on the mountain and largely Maronite. Its governor was Christian and had been nominated by Istanbul with the agreement of Britain and France. He ruled with a council formed on the basis of proportional representation: four Maronites, three Druze, two Greek Orthodox, one Greek Catholic, a Shi'ite and a Sunni. But as they really believed in the principle of a national state, the Lebanese soon began to struggle against the Ottoman system. (It should be remembered that it was the Lebanese, often Christians, who had first propounded the idea of the *nahda,* the Arab Renaissance, against the Ottoman Turks.) But strategic differences were already apparent: was Lebanon truly independent, or was it just an Arab kingdom within the Empire?

The Sykes-Picot agreement put an end to any such speculation. On September 1, 1920, one month after Faisal's defeat at Maysalun (see Chapter One) General Gouraud

In 1919 General Gouraud arrived in Beirut to set up the French Mandate. Before proclaiming the state of Greater Lebanon he had to defeat Faisal's followers who had made Damascus the capital of their Arab kingdom. The Arab nationalists would never forget: for them Lebanon was the fruit of colonial "sin."
Ph. © Collection-Viollet

proclaimed the State of Greater Lebanon. Overnight the surface area of Lebanon went from 4500 to 10,400 square kilometers. The addition of new territories was designed to help Small Lebanon's economic situation. But, more than that the very strong Christian majority (over three quarters of the population) in Small Lebanon was very much counterbalanced.

DENOMINATIONAL DIVISIONS IN 1920					
Maronites	176,000	31%	Sunnis	122,000	22%
Greek Orthodox	78,000	14%	Shi'ites	100,000	18%
Greek Catholic	40,000	7%			
Others	4,000	1%	Druze	40,000	7%
Total	298,000	53%	Total	262,000	47%

Christian Greater Lebanon had barely been proclaimed before it was already obsolete: the Christians were in danger of becoming a minority very quickly. The old Druze-Maronite axis became a minority (38%) as opposed to those of Byzantine orthodoxy and Muslims (Greek Orthodox Christians and Sunni) of which the total exceeded 42%. The redefinition of the borders also drew attention to the existence of the Shi'ite community who up until then had been more or less absent from the Lebanese political scene. They had been marginalized, chased off the mountain by the Druze, and had taken refuge in the area around Bekaa and the South where they were ruled over by feudal lords. Their sheer demographic weight made them the third largest group in the new country.

Externally, Lebanon was threatened by Syrian irredentism, as 1920 had been a catastrophic year for Syria, and Faisal's failure was directly linked to the proclamation of Lebanon. Situated at the heart of a cultural milieu which had both Mediterranean and Arab leanings, Syria was sorry to see its coastal access blocked by new partitions. In the north the Gulf of Alexandrette, the natural outlet of Aleppo, the second largest town in the country, was ceded in 1939 to Turkey by the French mandate. Above all (Beirut was only 120 km from Damascus), Lebanon was able to benefit from commercial transactions. But Syria seemed unable to deter a well-armed Israel who later occupied the Golan Heights, the key to Syria's Hauran plain, in 1967. After that, the "active" frontier between Syria and Israel moved from the Golan – which was militarily irrecoverable for Syria – toward the heart of Lebanese territory, where Syria had always wanted to "return": did not the Syrians and the Lebanese comprise "one nation in the two states?" Despite everything, Lebanon, quartered between France and the Arab world, between Christian insularity and Arab solidarity, became established thanks to a historic compromise between the Maronite Bishara al-Khoury, and the Sunni Riyad al-Solh, representatives of the two most important minorities. The 1943 National Pact confirmed that Lebanon was a country with an "Arab appearance." This peculiar form of words illustrated the double renunciation on which the Pact was based: the Christians were trying to do without French protection, and the Muslims were trying to renounce their Syrian or Arab ties; in 1950 Lebanon broke its customs union with Syria, and, in a liberal atmosphere, developed its service economy which was the foundation of its prosperity: imports from Europe, exports to the Arab world. Had Lebanon actually become a nation? As a journalist of the time quipped, "Two negations do not make a nation."

The great feudal Druze leader, philosopher and man of letters, Kamal Jumblatt, founded the Progressive Socialist Party. He led the opposition against Camille Chamoun in 1958, and joined in the civil war in 1975. After his assassination in 1977, in true feudal tradition, his son Walid succeeded him.
Ph. © B. Glinn/Magnum

The Pact also entailed the separation of powers between the communities: the Presidency of the Republic to the Maronite, the Presidency of the Council to the Sunni, the Chamber of Deputies to the Shiites, Foreign Affairs to the Greek Orthodox and so on. The pivotal axis became Sunni-Maronite rather than Druze-Maronite. Despite their historical importance the Druze were relegated to the sixth rank in the community.

In 1975, unable to lay claim to the Presidency of the Republic, Druze leader Kamal Jumblatt would lead a rebellion.

The Israeli-Arab Stranglehold

The 1956 war, and the resulting Nasserism, were at the origin of the first Lebanese crisis. The 1967 war and the establishment of the Palestinian resistance were to destroy the land of cedars. The defeated Arab

Against the backdrop of the Cold War, the Suez expedition reactivated Lebanese divisions. The "unionists" who were supported by the United Arab Republic, took up arms against President Camille Chamoun who refused to break ties with France and Great Britain. In July 1958, G.I.s disembarked on the beaches of Beirut to defend the beleaguered president.
Ph © B. Glinn/Magnum

world forced the Lebanese not only to support the new Palestinian refugees who were to swell the ranks of the 150,000 refugees from 1949 already in Lebanon, but also the Palestinian resistance war effort: Lebanon became an armed base for commando organizations. This "State within a State" was recognized by the Cairo Accords of 1969 between Lebanon and the PLO.

When the PLO was expelled from Jordan after Black September, it began to strengthen its bases in south Lebanon. In fact, the region actually came under PLO control: in "Fatah land" the Palestinians made the laws and subordinated the entirely theoretical sovereignty of the Lebanese state to their own national objectives. This intrusion in an unstable country hastened the overspill of tension. Just as the Arab countries did, Israel placed the consequences of the Palestinian resistance on frail Lebanese shoulders, declaring that it would hold any state responsible whose land was used as a base for terrorist activities. In 1968 in response to incursions from the south of Lebanon, *Tsahal* destroyed the Lebanese commercial airfield which was based at the Beirut airport. How could Lebanon prevent Israel, which had defeated Egypt, from violating its sovereignty? But, also how was it possible for Lebanon to prevent the Palestinian

CYPRUS: AN ISLAND CUT IN TWO

Situated opposite the Lebanese coast, the island of Cyprus was also influenced by the upheavals in the former Ottoman provinces of the Middle East. Cypriot nationalism which developed after the Second World War took an unusual form: the Greek community (around eighty percent of the population) led by the Ethnarch Makarios, who was both a patriarch and a political leader, did not claim independence, but *Enôsis*, union with the Greek motherland. The angry refusal of the Turkish minority (twenty percent) led to a compromise: the island's independence and minority rights would be guaranteed by Great Britain, the ex-colonial power, Greece and Turkey. However, the rivalry between the two Cypriot protectors led to tension: the Turkish Cypriots thought they had been wronged in the division of power, the Greek Cypriots still

dreamed of *Enôsis*, and criticized especially the paralysis which resulted from the tiny amount of local power allowed by the Constitution. On July 20, 1974 there was an attempted coup against Makarios which had been masterminded by the Greek colonels in Athens. This led to a massive intervention by the Turkish army. The northern third of the island was occupied, and Nicosia, the capital, was cut in two. This show of strength led to a massive exodus of people from one side of the "Attila Line" to the other (200,000 Greek Cypriots were displaced and 2,000 disappeared). Despite the repeated condemnations of the international community, Turkey did not withdraw from Cyprus. On the contrary, it set about modifying the demographic balance of the island by favoring the settlement of Anatolian peasants. Besides Ankara had

already proclaimed the Turkish Republic of Northern Cyprus in 1983, which it alone recognized.

In Cyprus, as in Lebanon, centrifugal forces and the intervention of external powers had divided communities which had coexisted for centuries. Churches abandoned in the north and mosques left derelict in the south bore witness to the reality of the partition, which the Cypriots, for the most part, had not wanted. But the search for a solution went further than Cyprus, to Athens and Ankara and even to Washington, since Greece and Turkey were both part of NATO. ∎

Ph. © Edimedia

resistance movement, "the honor of the Arab nation" from pursuing its struggle for liberation? A weak link in a regional chain, Lebanon, just like the Palestinians, was caught between Israel and the Arab countries. Some Lebanese resented the presence of the Palestinians, and nationalistic issues came into focus. The small Maronite population, scarred by the memory of their own persecution, refused to be integrated into a country in which they would be dominated. They set up "Maronitism" as a dogma: Lebanon belonged to them; it was not Arab. Denying all cultural evidence, many rejected their Arab status, and considered themselves "Phoenicians," – that is, "descendants of the Crusaders." This was how Israel became tempted to return to an exclusively Christian Small Lebanon. The Phalangists of Pierre Gemayel were very far from representing all those who were later to be collectively identified as the Christian camp – only nine of them were elected at the legislative elections in 1972. But nonetheless they began mass militia recruitment in the streets of East Beirut. Supporting war, they managed to appropriate nearly all Christian representation.

In April 1973, an Israeli commando operation assassinated three Palestinian leaders in the heart of Beirut. Tension went up a notch. It exploded in April

In Greater Beirut, those who were forgotten by the "Lebanese miracle" and in the grip of poverty shared the same sense of injustice as the Palestinian refugees. But, their problems were resolved within their close-knit communities. Slowly the struggle of the Palestinian progressives became confused with that of the Druze and Muslim militia (below Mourabitoun, Sunni partisans).
Ph. © Leroy/Gamma

1975 following a machine gun battle between Palestinians and Phalangists. The Lebanese Wars had begun, in the working class areas between Ain Romaneh (Christian) and Shiah (Palestinian and Shi'ite). Between 1975 and 1990 there would be 145,000 dead, 18,000 disappeared, and nearly 200,000 injured.

The Power of the Militias

The struggle for power took place in the very heart of each community. For example, hegemony in the Christian camp was secured in blood; in 1978, Tony Franjiyeh, one of the traditional feudal militia leaders, and his family and followers were murdered by the opposing Christian militias of Camille Chamoun. Later Chamoun's militia was crushed after extremely violent struggles.

Within the Shi'ite community, Nabbi Berri's Amal movement and the Iranian-trained Hezbollah struggled for control. While the Amal movement, which had ousted the Marxist left, fought for greater Shi'ite power within the Lebanese system through the construction of a new Maronite-Shi'ite axis, Hezbollah wanted to establish an Islamic republic which exactly reproduced the Khomeini model.

After Black September, the PLO, which was determined to defend its Lebanese sanctuary, armed its militants. The Christian camp was consumed with hatred for the Palestinian invader. Here were two nations in opposition: Bashir Gemayel was to recognize later that "there was one nation too many in Lebanon." Above, the burial of a Phalangist fighter in the heart of a divided Beirut.
Ph. © R Depardon/Magnum

The partisan involvement of the Lebanese favored the intervention of external players, basically Syria and Israel. In 1976 at the behest of President Suleiman Franjiyeh the Syrian tanks crossed the border. Below, a poster on a Paris wall in August 1978.
Ph © Roger-Viollet

Soon, the militia became actual armies which had at their disposal heavy artillery and sophisticated weaponry. The ephemeral 1985 accords between the Maronite Lebanese forces, Amal (Shi'ite) and the Progressive Socialist Party (Druze) attempted to address the fact that it was the militia, not the government, not even the classical political forces who held the real local power. On the other hand without the use of this powerful armed force, the voice of the smaller Sunni or the Greek Orthodox Christians would have been stifled during the long years of war.

Religious conviction, however, did not always guide political affiliation: some young Christians joined the ranks of the "Palestinian Islamic Progressives" and Muslims were to be found in the heart of the "Christian right." In the initial stages of the war some, including the secular left, fought for a particular idea of nation, and others for an ideal of justice. It was the

militia fighters who opposed the drift away from strict denominational identification. It is important to insist on this point: with the exception of a few extremists (the Maronite order of the "Guardians of Cedar" or the "Party of God" Hezbollah coming from the Shi'ite ranks), the Lebanese Wars were not wars of religion; they came about from a collision of socio-political and international conflicts in which the state, itself institutionally divided into castes, showed itself to be incapable of fulfilling its function as an arbitrator when faced with a major crisis.

Syrian Intervention

It was Suleiman Franjiyeh, Maronite President of the Republic from 1970 to 1976 who first appealed to Syria, because his "nationalist" camp risked being overwhelmed by the Palestinian-Druze militia, who were better able to handle their arms. Although Saika, the Palestinian militia, was actually pro-Syrian, Syria was nevertheless only too happy to seize the opportunity to intervene under the cover of an Arab dissuasion force. For the Damascus regime feared the "left" gaining victory, and were especially concerned by Yasir Arafat whose "Palestin-ism" sat ill with the Greater Syrian dream. Basically, in Franjiyeh's call for help Damascus saw the possibility of regaining a lost hegemony. The Syrian intervention in April 1976 marked a turning point in the war: it would serve as a pretext for the increasing number of Israeli raids which culminated in the invasion of Lebanon in 1978. From that point on, both Syria and Lebanon would invoke the presence of the other in order to justify its stance.

According to the historian Georges Corm, "the Lebanese territory and its people fulfilled the role of a symbolic space, like a boxing ring or a gladiator's arena, where the major players in the Middle East con-flict could confront each other, Soviets and Ameri-cans, Syrians, Palestinians and Israelis, Iranians and Iraqis, etc. Lebanon thus became a place of conflict which had a very important geopolitical function, for it

MARONITES AND DRUZE: MOUNTAIN SECTS

The historical alliance between the Maronites and the Druze, and their long peaceful coexistence, formed the basis of the Lebanese nation. The Maronites, who had believed for a while in monotheistic heresy, appeared in the fifth-century when they rose up against Byzantine Orthodoxy. Persecuted by Byzantium as well as by the Muslim Umayyads, they were the first to take refuge in the Lebanese mountains. They imposed their autonomy there and boasted of never having paid the *jizya*, the Muslim tax levied on the people of the Book. Despite their reintegration in the twelfth century into the heart of the Catholic Church the Maronites kept their own rituals. This feudal peasant people lived on the defensive and fiercely protected its own community. When faced with threats it often found allies in the Christian West, particularly in France, which was the inheritor of the Capitul-ations.

The esoteric Druze sect was also considered to be hereti-cal – by Muslims of strict Sunni persuasion. It was founded in the tenth century during the caliphate of al-Hakim, who had declared that Mohammad and Jesus were impostors and that he, him-self, was divine. Its followers, who were recruited from among the lower classes of Cairo, were persecuted and they also took refuge in the Lebanese mountains. Their dogma was complicated and had distinct gnostic elements – it was primarily characterized by a belief in the principle of universal reason, the *aki* pre-sent in every being. The secret is preserved in a com-munity which does not allow converts. As with the Shi'ites, persecutions have engendered the phenomenon of *taqiya:* the concealment of deep beliefs becomes a virtue.

Volney, a seventeenth-century French explorer, described how when the Druze "are among Turks they adopt Turkish customs: they go to mosques, carry out ablutions and pray. When they are among Maronites they follow them to church and drink holy water... so convincingly that they will finally die as neither Chris-tians or Muslims." Could this be seen as the beginnings of an Eastern Secularism? ■

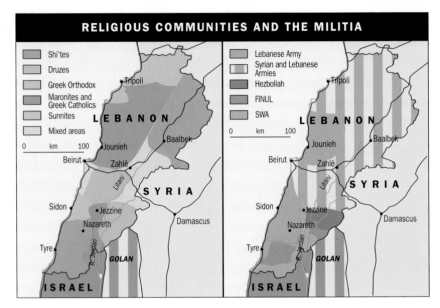

RELIGIOUS COMMUNITIES AND THE MILITIA

Left map legend:
- Shi'tes
- Druzes
- Greek Orthodox
- Maronites and Greek Catholics
- Sunnites
- Mixed areas

0 km 100

Tripoli
LEBANON
Baalbek
Jounieh
Beirut
Zahlé
Litani
SYRIA
Sidon
Jezzine
Nazareth
Damascus
Tyre
R. Jordan
GOLAN
ISRAEL

Right map legend:
- Lebanese Army
- Syrian and Lebanese Armies
- Hezbollah
- FINUL
- SWA

0 km 100

Tripoli
LEBANON
Baalbek
Jounieh
Beirut
Zahlé
Litani
SYRIA
Sidon
Jezzine
Nazareth
Damascus
Tyre
R. Jordan
GOLAN
ISRAEL

In 1975 (left hand map) the distribution of the different religious communities did not prevent them from being inextricably mixed all over Lebanon. Civil war and the stranglehold of the militia led to massive population transfers, and the creation of almost homogenous enclaves. In 1991 (right hand map), the community structure had altered radically.

allowed regional wars to take place without them turning into an international conflict. There have not been any significant Israeli-Arab wars since the beginning of the Lebanese conflict."

In fact the Lebanese civil wars fed off the financial and military support of countries in the region, who were in turn supported by the great powers (USSR, US, and France).

The circumstantial alliance between Syria and the Lebanese Forces could not last. Sadat's journey to Jerusalem in 1977 drew the Syrians and Palestinians closer together once again, and one year after the Damascus intervention the former allies were at war. While the superiority of the Syrian army imposed itself on the larger part of the territory, a small Christian stronghold in the hands of the Phalangist forces established itself in the north of East Beirut. Some Christians were tempted to take recourse to Israel, which was trying to eliminate the PLO bases in the south. In fact, when Major Saad Haddad created his own anti-Palestinian militia, the "South Lebanon Army," it was soon adopted, armed and supported by Israel.

In March 1978 Israel invaded South Lebanon and went as far as the Litani River, which had been claimed by the Zionist representatives at the Versailles Congress back in 1919 as Israel's "true frontier."

Following the Camp David Accords, the retreat of the Israeli forces from the Sinai on April 28, 1982, moved the conflict's center of gravity toward the north, where Israel was able to confront the Syrian and Palestinian forces with increased resources. At the same time Israel tightened its grip on the occupied territories. In May 1980 after an impasse in the Camp David-style negotiations on autonomy for the Palestinians, the Begin government revived the policy of Israeli settlements in the occupied territories; in December 1981 Israel annexed the Syrian Golan. The confrontation then moved to Lebanon where the PLO was still gathered.

In 1936, Pierre Gemayel (1905–1984) founded the Phalangists, who led the Christian camp thanks to the strength of their armed branch which was run by Bashir (1947–1982), Gemayel's son. Elected president on a program of national reconciliation just after the invasion of Lebanon, Bashir was assassinated twenty-two days later. His brother Amin (born in 1942) succeeded him. Ph. © Sygma

"Peace for Galilee"

On June 6, 1982, Ariel Sharon, the Minister for Defense in the Begin government, launched Operation "Peace for Galilee." The initial avowed objective was to repel the guerrillas who were threatening the north of the country forty kilometers from the border, but the government soon moved to eliminate all "physical or

symbolic pretenses, whether in military or organizational form" of the Palestinians in Lebanon. At the end of 1982, following a terrible two month siege and bombardment, Beirut mourned its tens of thousands of dead; as for the Palestinians living in the refugee camps in South Lebanon, 140,000 of them, (about two thirds) had to flee to Bekaa which was under Syrian control.

Confrontation between Israel and Syria then seemed inevitable. However, objective convergences existed between the two countries. First, tensions increased between Syria, which wanted to strengthen its hold on Lebanon, and the PLO, which wanted its logistical bases there. So anti-Palestinian concerns provided a basis for increased Israeli-Syrian cooperation. And from 1977 both the Syrian and Israeli forces had refrained from crossing the Litani River, an implicit "hot line." As those forces' rapport grew following the Camp David Accords, the line was pushed further north to the Beirut-Damascus road. The new "hot line" was more or less respected, even when Israeli troops retreated in June 1985. It was not until the Iraq-Kuwait crisis in 1990 that the balance of forces again shifted, this time in favor of new international acquiescence to Syria's role in Lebanon.

Just like the Western powers, Israel became bogged down in Lebanon. Despite American support it had not been able to impose a peace accord. Israel's invasion also helped engender the Shi'ite terrorist threat. Having fought Palestinian domination prior to 1982, the Shi'ites were to bitterly oppose the order imposed by Tel Aviv: this involved murderous guerrilla warfare, in which the Western hostages became embroiled, and which eventually contributed to Israel's partial withdrawal from Lebanon. The massacre of Palestinian civilians in the Sabra and Shatila camps, carried out by soldiers from the Lebanese Forces in an Israeli controlled zone, became the symbol of this "dirty war," whose purpose was even questioned within Israel. 400,000 demonstrators – ten percent of Israel's total population – expressed their disapproval. After achieving the withdrawal of Palestinian fighters, Israel withdrew

From 1970 President Hafez al-Assad ruled Syria with an iron hand. A committed Ba'athist, he was violently opposed to the Iraqi branch of the Ba'ath party led by Saddam Hussein. The Lebanese Civil War enabled him to regain a foothold in the country and to reaffirm Syrian pre-eminence. This policy led ultimately to the Taif Accords, and the Syrian-Lebanese Treaty of May 1991.
Ph. © Gamma

some troops while creating new "security zones" inside South Lebanon.

In September 1983, the Battle of Chouf found the Druze and Maronite militia at loggerheads. The Maronite defeat led to an exodus of Christians from this region to the south where the concentration of homogenous Christian villages made it possible to double the presence of the SLA in Israeli-occupied South Lebanon. These population displacements seemed to be an Israeli long-term strategy. In February 1982 a representative of the Israeli Ministry for Foreign Affairs declared: "The break up of Lebanon into five provinces... is already a *fait accompli*... The Druze

will establish their own state which will perhaps reach as far as our Golan, and certainly to Hauran (an area in South West Syria), a state that will guarantee the long-term peace and security of the region; this is an objective which is currently within our grasp." If such a plan was to happen the Ottoman succession finally would be settled, but at what price?

Israel's partial retreat (though it continued its occupation of a strip of South Lebanon), the inter-militia wars, and, above all, the failure of Gemayel's presidency, would precipitate the Syrian seizure of the country. Having reached the end of his mandate in 1990, Amin Gemayel refused to hold elections for his successor; that only added to the confusion. It served to divide the country and weaken the Christian camp. The Taif Accords ratified by the Lebanese government consecrated the Maronites' waning power and led to the Syrian Lebanese Accords of May 1991 which linked the destiny of the two countries.

While the "Peace in Galilee" operation succeeded in banishing the PLO from Lebanon, the net result was failure: the bloody siege of Beirut, and the Sabra and Shatila massacres badly affected the Jewish state's international standing, and strengthened the position of Israeli pacifists.

Ph. © S. Nachsbrand/Gamma

THE SHARING OF THE WATERS

In 1955 the joint problems of the exploitation of Jordanian waters and the construction of the Aswan high dam, precipitated the Suez Crisis. In a region which is constantly threatened with shortages, the proper exploitation of the waters is even more important today given the demographic explosion. Since 1953 Israelis and Arabs have been at odds over the sharing of the Jordan's waters, which in the north correspond to the armistice line. While Israel built penstocks capable of making "the Negev desert flower," Syria and Jordan planned to divert the waters to prevent their neighbor from benefiting from them. Following the Cairo Conference in 1964 when the Arab states decided to unify their efforts to thwart the Israelis, Levi Eshkol declared "any attempt by the Arabs to prevent Israel from using its part of the Jordanian waters will be considered by us as an attack on our territory." The aerial raid against the Syrian barrage in 1966 effectively contributed to the increase in tension which resulted in the Six Day War.

The subsequent unequal division of the water in favor of Israeli settlers, and to the detriment of the Palestinians has aggravated the situation in the Occupied Territories. From now until the year 2000 Israel's hydraulic deficit could increase by thirty percent; currently the country draws forty percent of its drinking water resources from the Territories (the West Bank, Golan and Gaza). Given Israel's current water shortages it is apparent that the restitution of the occupied territories would cause Tel Aviv yet further

problems. South Lebanon, concerned about the waters of the river Litani, also became involved in these "hydropolitics."

Egypt had a hydraulic deficit of twenty billion cubic meters. Despite the Aswan Dam which had reserves to last three years, the worst was only narrowly avoided in 1988. For this country, which today comprises nearly sixty million inhabitants, the management of the Nile has become an even greater necessity. Egypt has also been particularly concerned

by the political evolution of the countries which control the river upstream, principally Ethiopia and the Sudan: the planned building of some Ethiopian dams would have been a *casus belli*.

The Arab peninsula, which also suffers from chronic shortages, nevertheless produces ninety percent of the world's unsalted water. Diverse Pharaonic plans resurface from time to time: in the eighties it was the floating iceberg and in 1991 it was the "peace pipe," a giant pipeline which would irrigate the Arab peninsula from Turkey. Then Turkish barriers were built in South East Anatolia to store water "confiscated" from the Tigris and the Euphrates, much to the annoyance of Syria and Iraq. If the Ataturk project was a response to the need for development, it also included geopolitical considerations: the dams promoted a better control of this Kurdish region, because they encouraged the massive settlement of Turkish peasants. During the Gulf Crisis, Turkey brandished the threat of drought: its immense dams could drain the two major rivers of the Fertile Crescent. ■

The Syrian Bapka dam on the Euphrates.
Ph. © C. Salhani/Sygma

The *Pax Syriana* seemed to have been imposed, and on the international scene Lebanon systematically aligned her position with that of Syria, following Damascus into the peace process with Israel. It allowed the rebuilding of a Greater Beirut, which was finally free of militias, but Lebanon's size and weakness meant it had no choice but to ally itself with one of its more powerful neighbors.

After the Gulf War, Hezbollah, Shi'ites, Palestinians and Israelis all fought in South Lebanon. In December 1992 Tel Aviv provoked a major crisis in the peace process by expelling 415 Palestinian Islamists from the occupied territories into the no-man's land of Marj al-Zahour just outside its occupied zone in South Lebanon. In July 1993 Israel's shelling of South Lebanon forced the exodus of tens of thousands of people. In April 1996, reacting to shelling of the north of Galilee, Israel launched the "grapes of wrath" operation against Hezbollah, which led to the exodus of 400,000 Lebanese civilians. On April 18, the Israeli Army bombed a UN camp in Qana where several hundred civilians had sought shelter. The ninety-one deaths in Qana symbolized yet again the tragedy of Lebanon. This small country could not find a definitive peace or its independence without the resolution of its own institutional problems (democracy and minority rights) and the international problems (especially Israeli occupation and Syrian domination) for which Lebanon was the outlet.

During Lebanon's civil war Syria gradually came to play the role of political and military arbitrator between the different factions. And so in 1987 the Elite Corps of the Syrian army intervened to put an end to the disputes between the PLO, the Druze and the Amal movement who were fighting for control of West Beirut.

Ph. © A Taher/Gamma

WHAT IS THE FUTURE
OF THE MIDDLE EAST?

The 1991 Gulf War and the 1993 Oslo Accords upset the balance of power in the Middle East. The myth of Arab unity had been shattered, for the coalition against Iraq included, for example, both Syria and Israel. Since its military defeat, Iraq has remained subject to an embargo that has caused immense suffering for the people but has done little to move Saddam and his regime. Iraq's old enemy, Iran, also faced continued sanctions and US efforts to maintain its international isolation. As for Saudi Arabia, it came out of the Gulf War weakened: the guardians of the Holy places had revealed their total dependence on the US. Their policy of cheap and abundant oil benefited the US, at the expense of their OPEC partners. The attacks by Islamist forces on the US forces stationed in Saudi Arabia in 1995–96 underlined the weakness of the Wahhabite Kingdom and the growing resentment against it. Indeed, Osama bin Laden emerged from this background. Through the mutual recognition of Israel and the PLO, the Oslo Accord of 1993 aimed to end the belligerence between Israel and its Jordanian, Syrian, and Lebanese neighbors. On the same basis as the Camp David Accords with Egypt, its originators were trying to create suitable conditions for a regional common market.

Hafez al-Assad cashed in his chips for participating in the crusade against Iraq, and Syria got the green light to remain in Lebanon. The 1994 peace Jordan negotiated with Israel hastened the internal political evolution of the Arab countries. By calling for general mobilization against Israel, the Arab regimes had once been able to militarize their societies and muzzle their people. But with this brand of Arab nationalism defeated, a growing Islamist movement emerged. And as political Islam found itself closer to power, it was confronted with the challenge of modernity: Would the need for cultural and religious resources also make space for democracy? So far, the secular regimes have managed to survive, with Jordan and Syria ensuring their own "dynastic" successions, from Hussein to Abdallah and, from Hafez to Bashar. Also, democratic ideals have progressed: for all their flaws, the Palestinian Authority and its leader, Yasir Arafat, derive their legitimacy not from the armed struggle, but from the 1996 elections conducted throughout the territories.

By the end of the 20th century, it was not only the Arab-Israeli conflict that threatened to further destabilize the region. There was a demographic explosion, the increasing fragility of the oil economies, an increase in poverty, the proliferation of non-conventional arms. The incomplete dismantlement of Iraq's arsenal after the Gulf War reminded everyone of proliferation risks, and indeed, Iraq used chemical weapons against its Kurdish population in 1988. Despite the US creation of a Kurdish stronghold in the north of Iraq, despite the death sentence Turkey issued to the Kurdish leader Abdullah Ocalan and the Kurdish Workers' Party's (PKK) subsequent dissolution, the tragedy of this forgotten people continues.

As the nineties progressed and the century turned, discontent grew. The assassination of Yitzak Rabin by a right-wing Jewish extremist on November 4, 1995 was a turning point. Throughout the region extremists of every cloth seemed to be redoubling their efforts to derail the peace process. In Israel, the elections of Benyamin Netanyahu (1996–99) and Ariel Sharon (2001–) brought Oslo's fiercest opponents to the helm. Though "land for peace" was Oslo's basic tenet, since 1993, the settler population in the West Bank and Gaza has nearly doubled, to more than 200,000—not to mention another 200,000 Israeli Jews in East Jerusalem and its enlarged neighborhoods. These continuing "facts on the grounds," combined with failure of Clinton's efforts to strike a deal between Ehud Barak and Yasir Arafat, and Ariel Sharon's provocative visit of the Haram al Sharif (Temple Mount), precipitated the second intifada. The ensuing violence was symptomatic of Oslo's shattered hopes and resulting despair: waves of suicide-bombers spread terror in the Israeli population and triggered extraordinary reprisals, such as the destruction of the Palestinian Authority infrastructures by the Israeli army and the war crimes committed in Jenin in April 2002.

This happened, of course, in the shadow of September 11, 2001, with Sharon calling Arafat "his own bin Laden." Despite unanimous condemnation by the international community and a series of new, unimplemented UN resolutions (including an investigation of the Jenin massacres), Israelis and Palestinians were once again stuck in a bloody embrace.

Paradoxically, though, the very absurdity and dangers of the conflict might accelerate a new process of negotiation, since the root causes of the conflict and the parameters of a solution are now so obvious to the whole international community that almost everyone calls for an end to the Israeli occupation of the Territories and for two states, Israel and Palestine, living side by side. As the *New York Times* stated in May 2002, "settlements [are] the greatest Israeli obstacle to peace. They deprive the Palestinians of prime land and water, break up Palestinian geographic continuity, are hard to defend against Palestinian attack and complicate the establishment of a clear, secure Israeli border." Since the US, the EU, and other major players are now convinced of the need for a Palestinian state, perhaps the voice of the international community will prevail.

Yet, in considering the rest of the region, George Bush Jr. deemed both Iraq and Iran (along with North Korea) an "axis of evil." Indeed, ten years later, completing his father's unfinished business with Saddam seems very much in the cards for this President Bush. Will extremism or compromise hold sway in the Middle East? Despite the imperfections of an agreement like Oslo, such diplomacy remains preferable to violence, terrorism, and war. ■

■ Aruri, Naseer, *The Obstruction of Peace: The U.S., Israel and the Palestinians*: Monroe, ME: Common Courage Press, 1996.

■ Asali, K.J., *Jerusalem in History*, Northampton, MA: Olive Branch Press/Interlink, 2000.

■ Beit-Hallahmi, Benjamin, *Original Sins: Reflections on the History of Zionism and Israel*, Northampton, MA: Olive Branch Press/Interlink, 1993.

■ Bennis, Phyllis & Michel Moushabeck (eds.), *Beyond the Storm: A Gulf Crisis Reader*, Northampton, MA: Olive Branch Press/Interlink, 1991.

■ Chaliand, Gerard (ed.), *People Without a Country: The Kurds and Kurdistan*, revised ed., Northampton, MA: Olive Branch Press/Interlink, 1991.

■ Chomsky, Noam, *The Fateful Triangle: The United States, Israel and the Palestinians*, Boston: South End Press, 1993.

■ Curtiss, Richard, *Stealth PACs: How Israel's American Lobby Seeks to Control U.S. Middle East Policy*, Washington DC: American Educational Trust, 1990.

■ Fisk, Robert, *Pity the Nation: The Abduction of Lebanon*, New York: Atheneum, 1990.

■ Flapan, Simha, *The Birth of Israel: Myths and Realities*, New York: Pantheon, 1987.

■ Fromkin, David, *A Peace to End All Peace: The Fall of the Ottoman Empire and the Creation of the Modern Middle East*, New York: Avon Books, 1990.

■ Gee, John R., *Unequal Conflict: The Palestinians and Israel*, Northampton, MA: Olive Branch Press/Interlink, 1998

■ Hadawi, Sami, *Bitter Harvest: A Modern History of Palestine*, 4th revised ed., Northampton, MA: Olive Branch Press/Interlink, 1991.

■ Haddad, Yvonne Yazbeck, Byron Haines & Ellison Findley (eds.), *The Islamic Impact*, Syracuse: Syracuse University Press, 1984.

■ Hiro, Dilip, *Holy Wars: The Rise of Islamic Fundamentalism*, New York: Routledge, 1989.

■ Hiro, Dilip, *Iran Under the Ayatollah*, London: Routledge & Kegan Paul, 1985.

■ Hiro, Dilip, *The Longest War: The Iran-Iraq Military Conflict*, New York: Routledge, 1991.

■ Hiro, Dilip, *Sharing the Promised Land*, Northampton, MA: Olive Branch Press, 2002.

■ Hourani, Albert, *A History of the Arab Peoples*, Cambridge, MA: Harvard University Press, 1991.

■ Khan, Muhammad Zafrullah (trans.), *The Quran*, Northampton, MA: Interlink Publishing, 1997.

■ Lockman, Zachary & Beinin, Joel (eds.), *Intifada: The Palestinian Uprising Against Israeli Occupation*, Boston: South End Press, 1989.

■ Lynd, Staughton, Sam Bahour & Alice Lynd, *Homeland: Oral Histories of Palestine and Palestinians*, Northampton, MA: Olive Branch Press/Interlink, 1994.

■ McDowall, David, *Palestine and Israel: The Uprising and Beyond*, Los Angeles & Berkeley: University of California Press, 1989.

■ McGowan, Daniel & Marc H. Ellis (eds.), *Remembering Deir Yassin: The Future of Israel and Palestine*, Northampton, MA: Olive Branch Press/Interlink, 1998.

■ Mostyn, Trevor (ed.), *The Cambridge Encyclopedia of the Middle East and North Africa*, New York: Cambridge University Press, 1988.

■ Said, Edward W., *Orientalism*, New York: Pantheon, 1978.

■ Said, Edward W., *Peace and Its Discontents*, New York: Vintage, 1996.

■ Said, Edward W., *The Question of Palestine*, New York: Times Books, 1979.

■ Seale, Patrick, *Assad: The Struggle for the Middle East*, Los Angeles and Berkeley: University of California Press, 1989.

■ Sick, Gary, *All Fall Down: America's Tragic Encounter with Iran*, New York: Random House, 1985.

■ Sluglett, Peter & Marion Farouk-Sluglett, *Iraq Since 1958: From Revolution to Dictatorship*, revised ed., London: I.B. Tauris, 1990.

■ Woodward, Bob, *Veil: The Secret Wars of the CIA 1981–1987*, New York: Simon & Schuster, 1989.

5000 BC	First Mesopotamian cities.
3100 BC	First dynasty of the Egyptian Pharaohs.
1300 BC	Moses receives the Commandments.
334 BC	Alexander lands in Asia Minor.
146 BC	The Romans begin to expand into the Eastern Mediterranean.
AD 135	The final Jewish uprising is crushed.
622	Mohammed begins to preach; first year of the *hegira*.
632	Death of Mohammad.
638	Capture of Jerusalem.
651	Conquest of the Persian Sassanian Empire.
661	Martyrdom of the 4th caliph, Ali, founder of Shi'ism.
750–1258	Abysinnian caliphate in Baghdad.
969–1171	The break up of the Muslim Empire. The Fatimid caliphate in Cairo.
1099–1244	Crusades.
1453	The Turks capture Constantinople.
circa **1500**	Portuguese and then English enter the Persian Gulf.
1516	The Ottomans capture Cairo.
1535	Capitulations between François I and Suleiman the Magnificent.
1590	The Lebanese Emirate of Emir Fakhredine.
circa **1600**	Shi'ism becomes the official religion in Persia.
1638	The defeat of the Ottoman army in Vienna; empire begins to decline.
1744	The first Wahhabite state of the Saudi family in Arabia.
1798	Bonaparte's expedition into Egypt.
1830	The French Army captures Algiers.
1839	The British occupy Aden.
1840	The treaty of London ends Mehmet Ali's military aspirations
1860	The denominational massacres in Lebanon.
1869	The opening of the Suez Canal.
1875–76	Egyptian and Ottoman bankruptcy.
1875–77	Russian pogroms; first Zionist *aliya* to Palestine. Britain occupies Egypt.
1897	First Zionist Congress in Basle.
1899	Anglo-Egyptian control of Sudan. British protectorate in Kuwait.
1915	Armenian genocide.
1916	Sykes-Picot Accords. Sharif Hussein's Arab revolt.
1917	Balfour Declaration.
1919	The Wafd party demonstrates in Egypt.
1920	Defeat of Arabs at Maysalun: state of Greater Lebanon proclaimed.
1920–1922	Installation of the French and British mandates; creation of Transjordan.
1924	Mustafa Kemal Atatürk abolishes the caliphate.
1925	Reza Pahlavi ascends the throne of Persia.
1928	The Muslim Brotherhood movement is founded in Egypt.
1936–1939	Arab revolt in Palestine.
1943	National Lebanese Pact.
1945	Founding of the Arab League.
1947	The UN ratifies the Palestinian partition plan.
1948	Proclamation of the State of Israel; first Israeli-Arab War.
1949	Abdallah of Transjordan annexes the West Bank.
1951	King Abdallah of Jordan is assassinated.
1952	Coup d'état of the Free Officers in Egypt.
1954	Beginning of the Algerian War.
1956	Nasser nationalizes Suez Maritime Canal; Suez expedition.

1958	Iraqi revolution. The Americans intervene in Lebanon. Proclamation of the United Arab Republic (Egypt and Syria).
1960	Creation of Organization of Petroleum Exporting Countries (OPEC).
1962	Yemen War. Algerian independence.
1963	Ba'ath seize power in Syria.
1965	The first armed operation of Yasir Arafat's Fatah.
1967	First Israeli atomic bomb. Six Day War. Resolution 242 is ratified.
1968	Beginnings of Palestinian terrorism. The Ba'ath seize power in Iraq.
1969	The War of Attrition over the Suez Canal. Qaddafi's revolution in Libya.
1970	Black September. Death of Nasser.
1972	Munich massacre.
1973	Yom Kippur War; first oil crisis.
1974	Turkey occupies Northern Cyprus. Yasir Arafat is welcomed at the UN GA.
1975	Beginning of the Lebanese Civil War.
1976	The Syrian Army enters Lebanon.
1977	Sadat travels to Jerusalem.
1978	The fall of the Shah of Iran. First Israeli invasion of Lebanon.
1979	Camp David Accords. Second oil crisis; Soviet troops enter Afghanistan against the Mujahadeen.
1980–88	Iran-Iraq War.
1981	Israel annexes the Golan Heights. Israeli raid on the Iraqi central nuclear installation at Tamouz. Assassination of Sadat.
1982	Second Israeli invasion in Lebanon.
1985	The Israeli airforce bomb the headquarters of the PLO in Tunis.
1986	Civil war in Aden. The Americans bomb Libya.
1987	Beginnings of the Palestinian Intifada in the Occupied Territories.
1988	The PLO recognizes Israel.
1990	Taif Accords; surrender of General Aoun in Lebanon. Reunification of Yemen. Iraq invades Kuwait.
1991	Gulf War. The Israel-Arab peace conference opens in Madrid.
1992	Anti-Islamic military coup d'état in Algeria. Assassination of President Boudiaf. Mujahadeen capture Kabul.
1993	**September 13th** Declaration of Principles between PLO and Israel.
1994	Peace treaty between Israel and Jordan; Yasir Arafat returns to Gaza.
1995	Algerian opposition's "Rome Platform"; assassination of Rabin.
1996	First Palestinian general elections; Shimon Peres is defeated; violent Israeli-Palestinian clashes over Jerusalem.
1997	Israel begins new settlement in Arab East Jerusalem. Israeli–Palestinian (Oslo) negotiations broken off. Popular new president Mohammed Khatami elected in Iran, challenging hard-line clerics.
1998	Israel celebrates 50th anniversary of independence: Palestinians mourn 50 years of dispossession. US attacks Iraq in Operation Desert Fox; settlement expansion continues in Jerusalem. Wye River Talks.
1999	Geneva Convention meeting derailed. Barak elected Israeli prime minister.
2000	Camp David summit fails and second intifada begins.
2001	Ariel Sharon elected. September 11th attacks on World Trade Center and Pentagon. US launches "war against terrorism."
2002	Anti-terrorism war continues. Suicide bombers attack inside Israel. Israel launches major assault on Palestinian cities and refugee camps. UN calls for investigation of Israeli war crimes committed in Jenin.